Sneaky Fitness

Fun, foolproof ways to slip fitness

into your child's everyday life

With 50 all-new Sneaky Chef recipes!

BY MISSY CHASE LAPINE

Author of the bestselling book, *The Sneaky Chef*

AND LARYSA DIDIO

Enjoy!!

Missy Chase Lapine

RUNNING PRESS
PHILADELPHIA • LONDON

9 8 7 6 5 4 3 2 1

Digit on the right indicates the number of this printing

Library of Congress Control Number: 2009934054

ISBN 978-0-7624-3795-5

Cover design by Bill Jones

Interior design by Alicia Freile

Sneaky Fitness logo designed by Kristopher Weber

Edited by Jennifer Kasius

Front cover photograph of girl: istockphoto

Back cover photograph by Cathy Pinsky

Interior photography and inset on front cover by Jerry Errico

Food styling by Brian Preston-Campbell

Nutritional Analysis by Stacey B. Schulman MS, RD, CDN

Typography: Garth Graphic, Sassoon, and Zapf Dingbats

Running Press Book Publishers

2300 Chestnut Street

Philadelphia, PA 19103-4371

Visit us on the web!

www.runningpress.com

Medical Disclaimer: The ideas, methods, and suggestions contained in this book are not intended to replace the advice of a nutritionist, doctor, or other trained health professional. You should consult your doctor before adopting the methods of this book. Any additions to, or changes in, a diet or exercise program are at the reader's discretion.

Table of Contents

Snacks, Treats & Drink Recipes

PART ONE

CHAPTER ONE:

Keep Them Moving, Keep Them Healthy

"I spend all day helping people get into shape," says Larysa DiDio. "As a personal trainer, I had grand plans that my kids and I would exercise together. We'd take activity-filled vacations, and they'd literally jump at the chance to do something vigorous and fun. After all, I'm a physical fitness professional!"

But as every mother knows, once you actually have kids, they don't always behave in the way you daydreamed they would. One fine day in August, Larysa was feeling particularly confident in her maternal skills—her three-year-old son Nicholas was fed, well-napped, and contentedly sitting in the living room watching a movie. Then he turned to Larysa and asked, "Mommy, can I have some milk?"

"Honey," she said, "it's right in front of you on the coffee table." He shot her a frown that said, "Really? That's your answer?" then half-heartedly stretched out his arm to reach for the glass. The second his little fingers failed to reach the cup, he gave up. If he had lifted his bottom an inch, he could have grasped it, but that would have taken too much effort. Looking perplexed and not a little annoyed, he said, "Mommy, I can't reach it." So Larysa dropped the load of laundry she was carrying and went all the way across the room to push the glass two inches in his direction so he didn't have to exert himself.

A few days later, Nicholas was engrossed in his Leapster game cartridge while Larysa was briskly bringing some order to the household—straightening up and getting ready to do another load of seemingly unending laundry. "Nicholas," she said, "Jump up and throw your clothes in the hamper for me, please," thinking her exuberant little boy would gladly take her up on an excuse to move his energetic body. "Do I have to?" he asked her, barely looking up from his game.

Larysa was surprised and just a little bit panicked. "This was not the attitude I was expecting," she says.

While her son became a work-in-progress, Larysa decided she was going to start teaching her daughter Bella to be fitness-savvy early on and was delighted when she turned out to be energetic, enthusiastic, and full of pep. She was also a health-food junkie and would eat her fruit and veggies—even broccoli—with gusto. Larysa was excited and relieved. Raise a healthy little girl? Check!

Until she turned three, that is. "One day, Bella asked me for a piece of chocolate," remembers Larysa. "I explained to her that chocolate is a 'sometimes food' and that she could have one piece." Bella jumped for joy, and Larysa was pleased that her daughter had accepted this extremely reasonable boundary. She handed Bella the chocolate, watched her eat it, then went back to her task at hand. When Larysa turned around, Bella had left the kitchen and headed for her bedroom. This seemed odd, so Larysa followed her. "As I came in, Bella walked into her closet and closed the door behind her. Hmmm—more and more curious," Larysa thought. She gave her a couple of minutes, then opened the door. There sat Bella slowly unwrapping another piece of chocolate. She smiled sheepishly, chocolate all over her lips and chin, and said, "Mommy, I weally like chocolate!"

Sigh. Don't we all?

It's hard to impart the concept of health to a child, let alone convince one to embrace a lifestyle that leads to it. After all, the things that may motivate an adult, like fear of disease, warding off age, or vanity, aren't on kids' radar screens. It's harder still to convince children to make good-for-you activities like eating well and exercising regularly a habit— the more you nag or cajole, the more it seems like a chore, the more they'll dig in their heels, and the more you'll find yourselves battling each other. None of which leads to your original goal: showing your child how to embrace good health.

"I figured out fairly soon that I was going to have to struggle just as much as any other parent to keep my kids healthy and fit," says Larysa. Her one advantage was the numerous fitness methods that she had learned in the course of her professional training. "Still, after more than a few skirmishes, I discovered that you can bring a kid to the gym, but you can't make him sweat. I didn't want to browbeat them into it; I wanted them to want it. Something had to change."

ENTER SNEAKY FITNESS

One day, out of sheer desperation, Larysa pretended to be a deer and told her son to be the hungry bear and chase her. "I ran in front of him, just within reaching distance, and I did as much as I thought I could get away with. Far from tiring of it, he wanted to catch that deer and eat it! So he just kept running. It was the best workout he had ever had, and he was laughing the whole time," remembers Larysa. The next day Nicholas said, "Let's play the bear and deer game again." Never one to pass up a chance for exercise, Larysa happily gave in and it was another great workout for the both of them. "I felt a flush of hopefulness—my kid was begging to exercise. Was I onto something?"

Larysa began to get creative. "I had us run in locations where he had to jump over obstacles and sprint across ditches, which strengthened his body in new ways. He loved it and kept asking for more. Then I took it even further and reviewed the things he did every day, and found ways to ramp up their fitness factor— activities like searching for my keys (I lose them a lot), or 'pretending' we were lost when I was walking him home from school and having to take the long route. I played off his competitive spirit by racing him to finish ordinary tasks. I knew I was tricking him, but I have to say, I didn't feel an ounce of guilt. The more he moved his body, the better he felt and the more he wanted to play, er, workout," says Larysa.

Larysa felt like she had just invented the wheel, when one afternoon she came across Missy Chase Lapine's bestselling book, *The Sneaky Chef*. She was delighted to see that Missy was doing the same thing that she was doing with exercise, only with nutrition, and had organized it in an inventive, realistic, and completely appealing way. "We were the two major fronts of the same war—the battle to keep our kids healthy in a modern world that seems to work against us at every turn. I was even happier to discover what a success her sneaky method had become. This meant that she and I weren't the only ones who had these concerns, nor were we the only ones looking for solutions. If her book was on the *New York Times* bestseller list, it meant that thousands of parents all across the country were seeking to counteract the negative influences of a culture that lets kids slide into inactivity and then shames them for doing so because now they can't fit into skinny jeans," says Larysa.

When a mutual friend introduced Missy to Larysa, a partnership was born. "Applying the *Sneaky Chef* concept to fitness made perfect sense," says Missy, whose two daughters (a grade-schooler and a tween) also tended to lapse into bouts of inactivity. By hiding healthy foods in meals kids love, Missy has done more than just give moms the peace of mind that their children are getting the vital nutrients they need: She has helped declare a truce at the dinner table (no more fights over eating the broccoli on the plate) and has cleared the way for no-pressure, productive discussions about eating right (if they're not forced to eat the broccoli, it doesn't become a hot-button issue), all of which leads to instilling lifelong, good habits. Exercise, as Larysa discovered, can be camouflaged in the same way—with the same results.

As Missy points out: "In both nutrition and physical fitness, small changes have big benefits. What mother hasn't heard her kid yelling for her from another room? Even making a rule that you have to look Mom in the eye to talk to her will get kids moving more often—and instill good manners." The best part is that sneaky food is so delicious and sneaky activities are so fun that your whole family will want to get in on the act.

WHY YOU NEED TO SNEAK—NOW MORE THAN EVER.

Here is the great mystery of modern family life: Your kids' calendars are packed and your family never seems to rest, and yet, your children don't actually physically *move* all that much. There's an awful lot of sitting going on across America—sitting in front of video games, computer screens, televisions, and tiny cell phone screens. For kids of all ages, "play" happens in the den and not in the backyard. Exercise is becoming as antiquated as a VHS player.

Tweens can't tear themselves away from their cell phones, school-aged kids as young as kindergarten are buried under homework, and preschoolers are often plopped in front of a TV to buy a few moments of calm. Even those kids who play team sports on the weekends aren't exerting themselves all that much over the other five days of the week.

The result is that our kids aren't learning a crucial lesson: that exercise can give them more energy, improve their brain power, boost their self-esteem, make them stronger, and ward off health issues like obesity,

heart disease, and diabetes. Oh, and did we mention that exercise can actually be *fun*?

What makes this across-the-board lack of exercise alarming is that 32 percent of American children can be classified as being overweight, which may have long-term effects on their health, according to the latest research from the Center for Disease Control. Even more shocking is that many children are being forced to face the issue at an early age: almost one in five 4-year-olds is now obese, reports researchers at Ohio State University.

What's going on? Here are eight fundamental reasons why our kids may be facing weighty challenges:

1. Kids today are living a far more sedentary lifestyle than ever before. Television watching, Internet surfing, video game playing—pastimes that involve little exertion take up much of our children's days. And it's not just your text-message-addicted tweens that can't tear themselves away from a screen, either. Research shows even preschoolers spend as much as 90 minutes a day in front of a TV or computer screen, and that children's general activity levels start to drop between the ages of 3 and 5. Coincidence? Could be. But think of the last time you put off going for a walk to look up one last thing on the Internet or got distracted by your buzzing Blackberry.

2. **Public schools are facing huge budget cuts.** The lack of funding has hit many athletic departments hard, so there are fewer team sports in which to participate. Even more sobering: Many schools no longer require gym class every day, and some don't even let kids go outside for recess!

3. **Kids eat more fast-food meals.** In fact, the family sit-down dinner seems to be a quaint relic of the past. With demanding schedules for both parents and kids, sometimes there's no time to cook or gather as a family. Enter burgers-on-the-fly and drive-thru tacos.

4. **Our children are eating fewer and fewer fresh fruits and vegetables today.** According to the Institute of Medicine, children eat about 50 percent or less of the fruits and vegetables recommended by the government guidelines. Fresh foods—at home or school—can take longer to prepare than something in a can or out of the freezer case, and can sometimes also be more expensive.

5. **Processed foods are easy—but contain hidden health saboteurs.** They're quick, easy, and appealing to those of all ages, but prepared foods are typically over-processed, meaning they're higher in starch and fat. Even if you eat them in small portions, you still can be aiding and abetting weight gain. Not only that, but processed foods more often than not are cheaply made and contain ingredients like high-fructose corn syrup, which ranks high on the glycemic index, and monosodium glutamate (MSG), a flavor enhancer that can cause sodium levels to soar, which can lead to heart and kidney disease. In fact, 77 percent of our sodium intake these days comes from eating prepared and processed foods.

6. **Children and teens are drinking more of their daily calories.** Talk about a Big Gulp: Instead of reaching for a glass of milk or water, most kids ask for fruit drinks, sodas, and even coffee-based drinks, which have very few nutrients but plenty of calories.

7. Technology makes our lives easier, but it also makes us lazier. At the turn of the twentieth century, children had to burn a lot of calories just to continue the business of living. They were required to do more chores and had to walk wherever they wanted to go. In these overscheduled days, you'll be hard pressed to find a child who hikes to school—or has the time to go outside and play.

8. Portions are bigger than ever. Super-sized has become the norm, which makes it harder and harder to figure out what a single serving is just by looking at the food on your plate. If you've grown up in a world where bigger is always better, it's especially hard to estimate how much you are eating. Even snacks that seem as though they're packaged in single portions are very often two or three portions. And when was the last time your kid looked at the nutritional and serving suggestion information before tearing into a bag of chips?

It's not that kids don't want to be fit and healthy. It depends on the child, of course, but there are several impediments to instilling good-for-you habits in them, including:

- Kids are impetuous and impulsive. They just want what they want. They don't know how to set aside their desire for the ice cream cone *right now* in exchange for an ambiguous future benefit, such as low cholesterol.

- Kids don't want to make an effort to exercise unless there is an immediate and desirable goal. They don't make the effort to do something they don't want to do for a loftier cause. It has to be fun.

- Kids feel hopeless (this is especially true of preschoolers) when they don't see instant results for their hard work. Fitness takes time.

- Kids think of "exercise" as tiring and tedious, even though they're perfectly willing to wear themselves out on the playground.

- Kids would rather be doing other things, like playing videos or watching movies. Larysa has even heard kids say that exercise would be the last thing on their list "of every other thing there is to do in the whole wide world."

- Kids get into a habit of inactivity. They become lazy—and laziness begets laziness. After all, if you're out of shape, it's easier to get discouraged when you can't last out on the playing field. It becomes a vicious cycle that's incredibly hard to break.

So, other then asking your kids to drop and give you 20, what's a parent to do?

The Obesity Epidemic

It seems as though you can't turn on the evening news without a report on the obesity epidemic that's plaguing our children. According to the National Center for Health Statistics, the rate of obesity has increased by more than 7 percent for children aged 2 to 5, about 10 percent for 6- to 11-year olds, and more than 12 percent for kids aged 12 to 19. These children are at higher risk for heart disease, type-2 diabetes, asthma, and sleep apnea, as well as low self-esteem.

Not only that, but a recent study has found that obese teenagers have the same risk of premature death as those who smoke ten cigarettes a day. Researchers discovered that being overweight as a teenager increases the risk of dying before about age 60 by a third and being an obese teen doubles that risk.

The data is worrisome, but how do you know if your child is truly overweight? How do you know when to seek help? Your pediatrician will weigh your child at her annual checkup and will look at your child's weight in context. Is the weight gain consistent with her age? (She may be about to hit puberty.) Is his father an NFL lineman? (His heft may be his natural build.) However, if your child's weight has varied wildly from the year-to-year pattern, be sure to discuss it with your pediatrician.

THE SNEAKY FITNESS PHILOSOPHY

Just as *The Sneaky Chef* taught parents how to feed healthy food to their children in the guise of kids' favorite foods, *Sneaky Fitness* shows parents how to easily bring age-specific exercise into their children's lives without them realizing what's going on. You can let them spend some time getting to the next level of their favorite video game knowing that they've already gotten in some time flexing real-life muscles. After all, it doesn't matter how kids come to learn that moving their bodies makes them feel good, what matters is that they learn the lesson before it's too late.

Sneaky Fitness isn't gym class or another afterschool activity to schedule. Instead, it's a way to weave a cardio workout, strength training, and flexibility into your kids' everyday routines without them even realizing it. Just as in the *Sneaky Chef* books, we encourage parents to continue to teach and discuss healthy habits, including exercise. *Sneaky Fitness* aims to get your kids moving more, burning more calories, building more muscle, and generating more energy, all of which

will inspire a natural desire to do more. Once they get a "taste" of how good it feels to be more active, they'll be more likely to say "Yes!" when you ask if they want to sign up for a sports team or go for a family bike ride.

Take Marcie, a young client of Larysa's. The 12-year-old hated to exercise; it was almost as if she were afraid of it. "I tried my best with her," says Larysa, "but I couldn't get her to stand up, let alone break a sweat!"

Larysa persevered, however, mostly out of deference to Marcie's mother, who'd been a client for years. "I knew her mom was desperate. She was worried that if her daughter was this out of shape at age twelve, what would her health be like when she's eventually on her own?"

One day while Marcie sulked in the corner, Larysa, out of sheer boredom, balled up wads of old junk mail, struck the classic basketball pose, and aimed for the wastepaper basket. After about five minutes, she made it more difficult for herself by moving farther away from her makeshift target.

Marcie watched Larysa for a while, and then, suddenly, asked if she could try. Larysa tossed her the paper ball and said, "Sure. Here you go."

Marcie made the first eight shots without so much as touching the rim of the basket. This was fun! She kept going—all the way to her middle school gym, where she became the youngest point guard in the school's history—soon she was running from one side of the basketball court to the other, hopping, jumping, and waving her arms. Marcie was getting a great workout—but it didn't seem like *work*.

Then there was Tiffany. She was a chunky 13-year-old who was already starting to feel low about her body. Her mother wanted to help her improve her self-esteem before it got worse. Tiffany came to Larysa's studio with iPod buds in her ears and a sullen look on her face. Larysa asked her what she was listening to—and told her she also loved L'il Kim. In fact, she asked to hook Tiffany's iPod to Larysa's speakers so she could listen as well. They started to dance. Larysa did some intense moves. Tiffany, not to be outdone, followed her. Soon it was a game: Larysa would make a move, and Tiffany would copy it, adding another element. Dancing? Yes. Exercising? Absolutely. But Tiffany didn't find it a chore. "It was really fun for me, too," Larysa says.

Q: If they don't know they're exercising, how do we teach them to make it a habit?

A: They may not know they're "working out," but your kids will know how good it feels to play a running game outside with friends, to be able to carry a big box of blocks, or to be flexible enough to reach for a favorite T-shirt on a high shelf. Just because you're not letting them in on the secret doesn't mean you're letting them off the hook. Reinforce how good activity feels "Isn't that energy great?" "I'm so proud of how quickly you did that." "You must feel like Superman!". And, because you know they're burning the calories and flexing the muscles they need to, you can take the time to talk to your kids about the benefits of exercise without nagging or making it feel like just another "should" in their life.

The same sneak-up-on-you method also works for younger kids. When Tommy's school held its annual Presidential Fitness tests, the baseball-loving, athletic third-grader was embarrassed that he couldn't do push-ups or pull-ups, despite his skills on the field. So when he and Larysa met, she decided to give him another challenge. "Kids love contests," she says. "So I pulled out a copy of The Guinness Book of World Records and we found someone who, for example, jumped 255 times in one minute." She then challenged Tommy to see how many times he could jump in the same amount of time. With every challenge the contests helped him build his strength, agility, and stamina and by the time the next Presidential Fitness tests were given, Tommy not only improved his scores, but he also felt a huge sense of accomplishment.

A different victory was won with 4-year-old Claire, a friend's daughter, who preferred playing with her dolls to getting dirty in the backyard. "I had my dog Zoe with me," says Larysa, "and I asked Claire who she thought was faster, her or Zoe." They decided to find out. Claire raced alongside Zoe from one end of the backyard to the other, giggling the whole time. "Claire was elated and proud that she 'won' and turned to her mother to boast that she was 'faster than Zoe,'" Larysa remembers.

With *Sneaky Fitness*, kids of all ages and all personalities will discover how good it feels to get their blood pumping and muscles moving. They'll realize the confidence that comes from being strong and capable and will eventually not just embrace exercise as a vital part of their everyday lives but actually begin to crave it as well.

THE UPSIDE OF EXERCISE

Making exercise a habit isn't just about the numbers on the scale. Getting the move on has a multitude of benefits for kids now and in their future:

- *More energy.* The heart pumps oxygen-rich blood much more efficiently—which translates into energy.
- *Fewer sick days.* Research shows that exercise strengthens the immune system, which in turn keeps kids from getting sick.

- *Improved mood.* Studies show that regular exercise releases mood-enhancing chemicals like endorphins.

- *Better self-esteem.* The confidence that comes from having a strong, toned body can translate into better body image.

- *Increased brain power.* The latest research on exercise shows that it improves mental acuity—well into old age.

- *Consistent weight control.* Simply put: Exercise burns calories. And if kids burn more calories than they consume, they'll lose weight.

- *Stronger muscles and bones.* Children are still developing—which makes it vitally important that they build bone tissue and muscle mass. Exercise is the way to do just that.

- *Better sleep.* When children do some form of exercise after school, the natural dip in body temperature that occurs five or six hours later may help them fall asleep—and sleep better.

- *Reduced risk of diabetes and cardiovascular disease.* Hundreds of studies show that exercise can help lessen the risk of heart disease and type-2 diabetes. The earlier a person starts to make exercise a habit, the less of a risk these chronic diseases become.

- *Fewer injuries.* Exercise helps foster flexibility and range of motion. A child who exercises is literally more resilient.

- *Better grades.* IQ might have a lot to do with heredity, but studies also show that exercise stimulates the formation of new brain cells, especially those responsible for memory and learning.

Missy and Larysa are real moms with real kids, who are faced with the same challenges as you when it comes to keeping their children healthy. Their days are filled morning to night with homework, after-school activities, jobs, walking the dog, grocery lists, and more. There's not enough time to do everything. Luckily, they've figured out some real, doable solutions that don't take much time and show results fast. Together, they'll easily help you get your family to the starting line for a vigorous and vibrant life. Ready? Set? Go!

CHAPTER TWO:

The Game Plan

A body in motion tends to stay in motion—it's not just a physics lesson, it's also the key to *Sneaky Fitness.* "It's hard to overcome inertia—to go from zero to sixty on the active scale," says Larysa. Instead, *Sneaky Fitness* gets your child in the habit of moving, building muscles, increasing stamina, and developing a craving for that post-exercise energy without even realizing it's happening. This chapter will outline the stealth strategies this book uses to launch your favorite little bodies into healthy motion.

Sneaky Strategy #1:
KNOW YOUR AUDIENCE

First, because what will charm your pre-schooler will most likely elicit bored rolls of the eyes from your tween, and because what a grade-schooler can manage without a second thought may prove frustrating for littler kids, *Sneaky Fitness* will indicate what activities tend to work best for what ages. To make things easier, we've grouped them into three age categories:

• Preschoolers (ages 2–4)

• Grade-Schoolers (ages 5–8)

• Tweens (ages 9–12)

Kids' personalities, interests, and capabilities change as they grow. Knowing what makes your kid tick will help you figure out how to motivate him. Here's a short guide:

PRESCHOOLERS

Parents of preschoolers rejoice—your little ones are at the perfect age for building healthy fitness habits. First of all, they are just about bursting with natural energy. Larysa had so much of it when she was that age that her mother used to look at her in wonder and say, "You must have eaten some kind of magic beans. How can you run up and down that hill and not be out of *breath?*" Larysa would shrug and take off running again.

Secondly, because they're naturally active, it will be easier to convince your preschoolers to join you in the activities described here. They are, for the most part, blank slates when it comes to moving their little bodies and haven't yet formed any negative associations with exercise. Nor have they time to develop much affinity for sitting on the couch. In short, they're perfectly primed for making fitness not only a part of their day, but a part of their future.

That said, preschoolers are often overly intense about their play, so you may have difficulty tearing them away from, say, building blocks and knocking them down again and again. The good news is that they are also easily distracted, so as soon as you present another fun option (like catching fireflies), they'll quickly be on board.

Physically, a preschooler's large muscle control is more developed than their small muscle control. They run, jump, and balance with confidence, but activities involving fine detail—or ones that take longer than a few minutes—will frustrate them. Take it from Larysa, mom of preschooler Bella: because preschoolers have a short attention span, it's best to go from activity to activity for as many times as your child is willing—and for as long as you can keep up with them!

GRADE-SCHOOLERS

If there's ever an age where kids like to plot and plan, it's 5 to 8 years. Missy's daughter Sammy and Larysa's son Nicholas are squarely in their grade-school years, so we know that unlike preschoolers, grade-school schemers are interested in real-life tasks and activities—and have the attention span to see most of them through. They love to be "in" on things (so if you slip up in your sneaky ways here and there, don't worry, chances are they'll jump at the opportunity to help you pull the workout wool over someone else's eyes—especially a younger brother or sister). They are cheerful and creative, constantly cooking up their own games and stories. They'll be pleased to offer you plenty of suggestions on how to tackle a job and will more likely than not entertain you with a running commentary as you go. Grade-schoolers like nothing better than to get a friend involved or to be part of a group. They're also becoming more competitive and are always eager to test their strength and skill, measuring themselves against you, siblings, and classmates. All of which adds up to a group of fun and enthusiastic kids.

Still, there are some challenges for parents of grade-schoolers. Now that your children are out in the wider world—their classroom, their friends' houses, the playground—you have less and less control over their activities, and less-than-desirable (from your point of view, anyway) preferences start to creep up ("But Mom, Jimmy has a TV in *his* room.") Kids this age start to be-

come computer-centric and, if left to their own devices, will spend hours in front of a screen playing games or using interactive toys that have an online component. Television programs geared to the after-school hours tempt them (especially since they no longer need you to turn on the tube). And homework starts up for real, meaning they spend even more time sitting still.

Physically, grade-schoolers are adept at both gross and fine motor skills, and their strength and muscular coordination improve rapidly—so don't be surprised if you suddenly find yourself having to keep up with *them*.

TWEENS

It seems as if it happens overnight—your adorable grade-schooler comes home with a new language, a new attitude, and new opinions on *everything*. Welcome to years 9 through 12, otherwise known as the "Tween" years. Not quite little kids, not quite teens, these in be*tween* years are in many ways the most crucial for setting your child up for a healthy adulthood. After all, this is when kids become the most sedentary. *The Journal of Pediatrics* agrees: A 2006 study found that the Tween years are the most critical in a child's life, and lifestyle choices made during this time will affect them for the rest of their lives. This is when lifelong habits form, meaning that we parents need to help them form the right ones now.

Of course, though tweens start to push boundaries, if they think you're pushing something on them, they'll promptly turn in the opposite direction. That's why our sneaky methods will become an essential weapon in your get-healthy arsenal.

Right about now you've realized that it has become increasingly harder to get your tween motivated to get moving. Technology has entered their world in almost an omnipresent way. Texting and IMing, video games and fan sites, email and DVR—

What Your Kids Burn Everyday

It's sometimes difficult to estimate how many calories you burn doing everyday things. The list below will give you a benchmark (calculated for 60 minutes of activity and for a 60-pound child). The numbers are clear: sitting in front of the computer or television generates as much energy as sleeping, and weaving daily activities into your child's routine can make a big difference.

Sleeping: 25 calories

Watching television: 27 calories

Typing on the computer: 41 calories

Light housecleaning: 68 calories

Playing frisbee: 81 calories

Walking: 90 calories

Raking the lawn: 117 calories

Light Dancing: 122 calories

Carrying wood: 136 calories

Skipping: 136 calories

Skateboarding: 136 calories

Digging in the backyard: 136 calories

Shoveling snow: 163 calories

Riding his or her bike: 218 calories

Jogging: 218 calories

Stair stepping: 245 calories

Jumping rope: 272 calories

tweens are adept with and ardent fans of them all. Their social lives becomes less about "play" and more about "hanging out." And while they're not full-fledged moody, moping teens, it's more challenging to get them to get up and go than ever before. Unfortunately, it's a vicious cycle. The more your child is sedentary, the more he or she will want to be sedentary and the more they'll resist when you try to push them. The tween years also coincide with the beginning of puberty, meaning your child's bodily changes can be varied and rapid. Tweens now have the ability to put on muscle mass. He or she may feel "gawky" and uncoordinated. This means you'll have to be sneakier than ever. Luckily, Larysa has specialized in training tween-age kids for 10 years. Her secret is to tap into the activities your kid loves. (It worked for Emily, Missy's tween daughter!) Trust us, once you get a tween interested in something, they will focus all their attention on it. (If you've ever seen a tween talk about *High School Musical* or *The X-Men*, for example, you'll know what we mean). Find something they love, and tweens will not only stick with it, they'll beg you to do it. Neat, isn't it?

Larysa's other tried-and-true tween trick is to make your middle-schooler think that it's not about them, it's about you. Tell them you want to get back into shape or eat right or learn to dance or take up yoga, and ask them for help by going for a walk with you, helping you make healthy dinners, or going to a class with you.

No matter how old your kids are, the bottom line is: Know your child. Find out what brings a smile to his or her face (spending time with Mom, helping out Grandma, finding the latest tunes for his or her iPod) and adapt these ideas to what they already love. Remember: A happy kid is usually a healthy kid.

Sneaky Strategy #2:
FIT FITNESS INTO THEIR EVERYDAY LIVES

We know how busy you and your kids are: There are errands to run, chores to finish, places to go, people to see. Oh, and did we mention homework to be done, friends to hang out with, toys to play with, and choruses of "I'm bored" to find time for? But instead of looking at your to-do list as a chore or your everyday as humdrum, we aim to help you seize many of these moments as unique opportunities to work in some exercise. In fact, each of these sneaky tips is designed for you to easily slip into your family's regular routine. And because we know your free time is in short supply, we've highlighted the heart of each tip so you can get to it fast. Have more time? We've given you "supercharged" add-ons to give the activities an extra oomph. Flip through and find your favorites.

Sneaky Strategy # 3:

REMEMBER—EVERY BIT COUNTS

Each activity we suggest will give your child a mini cardiovascular, strength, flexibility or agility workout and will also provide an opportunity to burn extra calories—and we'll show you just how many. **Throughout the book, our calorie calculations are for a 60-pound child, the average weight of a grade-schooler. If your child weighs 30-pounds (the size of a typical pre-**

schooler), halve the caloric expenditure; if he or she weighs 90 pounds (the typical tween), increase the calories by 50 percent. The numbers may look small, but it's important to know that every little bit counts. For example:

If you. . . Take the stairs, instead of the elevator, you'll burn an extra 36 calories in 10 minutes.

If you. . . Jog to your car and back instead of walking throughout the day, you'll burn an extra 31 calories per 10 minutes

If you. . . Dance after dinner instead of watching a 30-minute sitcom you'll burn an extra 47 calories.

. . . which adds up to a total of 163 calories. And that's just for starters. The Sneaky Fitness methods will help you sprinkle these calorie-burners throughout your child's day. Beyond that, you'll also be squeezing in heart-healthy cardiovascular workouts, metabolism-boosting muscle builders and ways to increase your child's flexibility, which will have him or her feeling energized and capable. It also adds up to more quality time with your child as you play your way through the mood-boosting activities together. It's a windfall for your child's physical fitness and for your family's happiness!

Sneaky Strategy # 4:
MOTIVATE WITHOUT SAYING A WORD

Sometimes the less you say, the more of an impact you make. Keep some simple fitness tools around the house and let your children "discover" them. Leave a mini-trampoline in the TV room and see how long it takes them to bounce during their favorite show. Hang a stopwatch in the garage and see how quickly they start timing how fast it takes

Equipment that every active family should have

- ■ Stopwatch
- ■ Jump rope
- ■ Mini trampoline
- ■ Pogo sticks
- ■ Sidewalk chalk
- ■ Bosu®
- ■ Hula hoops
- ■ Balls (basketball, rubber, NERF®)
- ■ Hippety hop ball
- ■ Stability ball
- ■ Hacky sac®
- ■ Bikes & scooters
- ■ Rain gear (so there will be no excuses to stay inside!)

We've also included a more extensive list of fit toys for all ages in the Appendix.

Dietary Recommendations for Children

Ever wonder if the plates you're putting in front of your kids are well-balanced? We did too. Here are some guidelines from the American Heart Association.

AGES 2 TO 3 YEARS

Fat: 30 to 35 percent of daily calories

Milk and dairy: 2 cups

Lean Meats and beans: 2 ounces

Fruits: ⅓ cup to 1 cup

Vegetables: ⅓ cup to 1 cup

Grains*: 3 ounces

AGES 4 TO 8 YEARS

Fat: 25 to 35 percent of daily calories

Milk and dairy: 2 cups

Lean Meat and beans: 3 ounces (girls); 4 ounces (boys)

Fruits: 1 cup (4 year olds); 1½ cups (age five and up)

Vegetables: 1 cup (girls); 1½ cups (boys)

Grains*: 4 ounces (girls); 5 ounces (boys)

AGES 9 TO 13 YEARS

Fat: 25 to 35 percent of daily calories

Milk and dairy: 3 cups

Lean Meat & Beans: 5 ounces

Fruits: 1½ cups

Vegetables: 2 cups (girls); 2½ cups (boys)

Grains*: 5 ounces (girls); 6 ounces (boys)

AGES 14 TO 18 YEARS

Fat: 25 to 35 percent of daily calories

Milk and dairy: 3 cups

Lean Meat and beans: 5 ounces (girls); 6 ounces (boys)

Fruits: 1½ cups (girls); 2 cups (boys)

Vegetables: 2½ cups (girls); 3 cups (boys)

Grains*: 6 ounces (girls); 7 ounces (boys)

*At least half of daily grains should be whole grains

them to run up and down the driveway. Really, you can't get sneakier than that!

Sneaky Strategy # 5:
SERVE SNEAKY CHEF HEALTHY BITES

Busy bodies need healthy fuel. Luckily, Missy has developed dozens of new *Sneaky Chef* recipes that are designed to give your kids energy that lasts all day by using slow-burning ingredients. High-sugar foods, such as refined sugars, and carbohydrates such as white bread and pastas, make your blood sugar soar, and may give you a quick burst of energy. Unfortunately, your blood sugar tends to drop just as quickly, leaving you feeling lethargic and hungry. Complex carbs, like whole grains, and proteins like beans and legumes, on the other hand, take longer to digest and therefore keep your blood sugar, appetite, and energy level on an even keel, which is why we utilize them here as much as possible. And, as with Missy's other books, these dishes disguise their healthy ingredients, so kids will reach for seconds.

GYM BAG OF TRICKS

Your covert coaching can be made easier if they're done alongside these tricks:

1. **Limit screen time:** The American Academy of Pediatrics recommends that you limit the time your child spends in front of a television or computer to no more than 1 to 2 hours a day. The best way to make that happen? Plan what you and your child will watch ahead of time, and limit your own time on the couch. Little monkeys see, little monkeys do!

2. **Make sure they're getting their zzzs:** Not only will it be hard to motivate bleary-eyed bodies to move, but a lack of sleep wreaks havoc on hormone levels, which in turn can lead to weight gain. A good night's sleep also keeps kids healthier and motivated to work out.

3. **Make it fun:** Remember, if it seems like a chore, it will be, so be sure to laugh along with them when you're exercising with your kids, and when you're on your own, make sure you're doing something you love, too. Your whole household will be happy—and healthy!

4. **Drop some hints:** Don't be afraid to point out in the middle of an activity how great your child feels and the skills he's mastered ("You're such a good balancer!" "You never run out of steam!" "Look at how much confidence you have"). Your words of encouragement will reaffirm his positive feelings toward exercise.

5. **Have them dress the part:** All the exercise in the world won't do anyone much good if they're injured, so make sure their sneakers fit and their clothes are appropri-

How Parents Can Lend a Healthy Helping Hand

1. You may think that your child's only hero is Hannah Montana, but in actuality, her true hero is you. So make like a role model and be sure that when you work out you don't complain about it. After all, how many times have you heard her mimic your exact words?

2. Emphasize not just the importance of exercising and eating well, but also the effects of doing so—that you feel strong, full of energy, and happy after coming home from the gym or polishing off a delicious bowl of berries.

3. If you want your child to have a healthy body image, then you have to have one, too. Try not to focus on weight loss when you talk about your workouts and diet, or when you are trying to get them to eat healthfully too. Refrain from criticizing their body and yours.

4. Participate! We know you're busy. We are too. But when your child asks you to go outside to throw a ball around or for help building a fort in the backyard, take them up on their offer. Chances are, you'll get many more like it.

ate for the activity at hand. Keeping equipment on hand, like a pair of sneakers in your car or a ball in your bag, will keep things spontaneous and will nip any exercise excuses in the bud.

6. **Keep their stuff in good shape.** Make sure your kids' sports equipment or exercise tools are organized and in good condition. There's nothing worse than when your child is excited to hop on his bike only to find that a tire is flat. Talk about deflating enthusiasm! Especially if he ends up shrugging his shoulders and heading inside to watch TV instead.

Most importantly, the *Sneaky Fitness* team has made the program easy to use. "It's not an all-or-nothing thing—even 10 minutes of exercise makes a difference," says Larysa. Just open the book to any page, lace up their sneakers, and start the fun!

A KEY TO THE ICONS

Whether you want your kids to better their balance or fit in more fiber, our activities and recipes will help you meet your family's healthy goals. These icons will help you map out where to start.

Cardiovascular Endurance: Strengthens the heart's ability to pump blood, which fuels the muscles— and the brain. Plus, it burns lots of calories!

Strength: Develops muscles so kids can exert the power they need to be effective every day, increases kids' metabolism (meaning they burn more calories while resting), and helps them avoid injury.

Balance: Controls the body's position when stationary (like when in a handstand) or when moving (like on the balance beam), which helps concentration and assists them in doing everyday activities.

Flexibility: Allows kids' bodies to move in an extended range of motion, helps avoid injury, and relaxes them!

Coordination: Helps their muscles function in a harmonious way and will assist in developing gross motor skills.

Mood Booster!: Gets their heart pumping and their muscles moving so their brains get a big dose of endorphins. Plus they get a host of confidence from being able to perform with grace and strength. All of which adds up to a great mood!

CHAPTER THREE:

Sneaky Fitness Quick Ideas!

Whether you have only a few minutes or a full weekend, *Sneaky Fitness* has ingenious ideas for slipping some exercise into your kids' day—without them noticing. We've disguised these ideas in "fun", weaving them through the activities your children already enjoy.

We'll tell you what you need for each idea (most often things you already have handy), what age the exercise is most suitable for, how many kids it takes to play, and when the optimal time to play it is. These are, of course, guidelines, not hard-and-fast rules, so you can adapt them as you see fit (pun intended!).

These covert ideas are accompanied by the estimated calories your children will burn as they do them. As a reminder, we've calculated the calories for a 60-pound child. If your child weighs 30 pounds, halve the caloric expenditure; if he or she weighs 90 pounds, add 50 percent more.

Each activity suggests a Sneaky Supercharge, which is an additional variation that will challenge your kids just a tiny bit more and help to keep older kids engaged in what their younger siblings may be doing. This fitness boost will extend the time your child moves and will require her to use a little more coordination, balance, agility, or core strength.

Start from the beginning or flip through—the exercises are ordered by age from what will appeal to a preschooler to tweens. However you start your secret mission, your kids will be having so much fun, they won't figure out they're also building healthy habits.

Q: How can I make my preschooler kick the stroller habit?

A: We've got five easy steps for convincing your child to put one foot in front of the other:

1. Get him interested in finding things along the way—if he can't see objects closely, he'll be forced to get out of the stroller and explore.

2. Make traveling to and fro fun by asking him to skip, hop, or jump to your destination.

3. Give him a sense of accomplishment by helping him count his steps.

4. Pretend the stroller is broken. (We're only half kidding.)

5. Have him push his favorite stuffed animal around in the stroller.

#1: Marching Band

You don't need seventy-six trombones to lead a big parade. All you need are some willing band members and some imagination. The music you make may not hit the top of the charts, but the exercise you're sneaking in is solid gold.

What you'll need: Musical instruments, or make your own with pots and pans, beans in a coffee can, a plastic container filled with water, or upside-down buckets

Who's playing: Preschoolers

How many: 2 or more

Prime time: Any Day, Weekends, Playdates, Parties

Lead your "band" around the house and/or outside, and up and down stairs, reminding them to march by bringing their knees up high as they go.

• • • • •

FITNESS FACTOR: Cardiovascular Endurance, Coordination, Mood Booster!

COVERT CALORIES: Marching will burn 53 calories in 20 minutes.

SNEAKY SUPERCHARGE: Have them step side-to-side for one minute, skip for one minute, walk backward for one minute, and jump for one minute as you make your way through the parade route. You'll tack on an extra 72 calories.

Fun fact! The instrument that burns the most calories is the drum—twice as many as playing wind and horn instruments.

#2: Dig to China!

While you're weeding the garden or shoveling snow, arm your child with a bucket and a child-sized shovel and she will be happy to dig for hours!

What you'll need: A child-sized plastic shovel and a bucket

Who's playing: Preschoolers

How many: 1 or more

Prime time: Sunny Days, Weekends

Set your child up in a garden patch or in a small pile of snow. Tell her to dig down as far as she can and if she digs far enough she may just reach the other side of the globe. Keep her interest by asking what she thinks she'll see when she gets there and what she'll say to the people she meets.

FITNESS FACTOR: Strength, Cardio

COVERT CALORIES: She'll burn 68 calories in 30 minutes.

SNEAKY SUPERCHARGE: Have her fill the bucket with dirt or snow and dump it into a pile a few feet away. For added incentive, offer to time her to see how fast she can fill 5 buckets.

Fun fact! If you actually dug a hole through the globe from anywhere in the United States, you are almost guaranteed to hit water on the other side of the globe, not China.

#3: Window Washer

What's better than making a big mess? Making it with shaving cream, of course. Keep in mind that your windows may not end up as streak-free as you would like, but the fact that your child is moving and stretching will be crystal clear. (At least to you, anyway.)

What you'll need: Shaving cream or colored soap crayons (made for use in the bath-tub), sponges, squeegees, water bottles, and buckets

Who's playing: Preschoolers

How many: 1 or more

Prime time: Sunny Days, Weekends

Let your little Michelangelo spray shaving cream or use colored soaps to draw on the outdoor side of a sliding glass door. Then hand him a bucket of water or water bottle, sponges and/or a squeegee to wash it off.

FITNESS FACTOR: Cardio, Flexibility Mood Booster!

COVERT CALORIES: He'll burn 27 calories in 20 minutes.

SNEAKY SUPERCHARGE: Don't let the rainy day deter you—just head to the bathroom and use the shower walls instead. Or, have him wash the windows of your car which will have him walking and stretching further.

SAFETY PRECAUTIONS: Keep a close eye on any bathroom "cleaning," as it's easy to slip in a soapy shower. Also, steer clear of menthol shaving cream, which can burn eyes.

#4: Parachute Party

You don't need to go to a class or rec center to play with a parachute—all you need is a sheet and a willing kid!

What you'll need: A clean or heading-to-the-washer sheet, a soft ball

Who's playing: Preschoolers

How many: 1 or more

Prime time: Any Day, Rainy Days

Place the ball in the middle of the sheet. Have your child take one end of the sheet while you take the other. Lift the sheet to get the ball into the air. See how many times you can make it bounce.

FITNESS FACTOR: Cardio, Coordination, Strength, Mood Booster!

COVERT CALORIES: She'll burn 36 extra calories in 20 minutes.

SNEAKY SUPERCHARGE: Snap the sheet and challenge her to roll under it before it lands on her. See how many times she can do it without getting "caught."

#5: Balloon Bash

Who needs a candy-filled piñata? Our version is healthier—and cheaper!

What you'll need: A blown-up, non-helium balloon for each child, a Wiffle ball bat

Who's playing: Preschoolers

How many: 1 or more

Prime time: Sunny Days, Playdates, Parties

Place an inflated balloon on the lawn and see how long it takes him to pop it using only a Wiffle ball bat. (Optional: If you squirt shaving cream in the balloon, it will explode when it's hit, which makes for some messy fun!)

FITNESS FACTOR: Strength, Cardio, Coordination, Mood Booster!

COVERT CALORIES: He'll burn more than 68 calories every 30 minutes!

SNEAKY SUPERCHARGE: Challenge him to hit the balloon in the air like a baseball before popping it on the ground.

SAFETY PRECAUTIONS: Be sure to pick up and throw out any pieces of the popped balloon as they can be a choking hazard to young children and animals.

Active Party Ideas for Preschoolers

Your life may already feel like a three-ring circus, but setting up a pretend Big Top in your yard or house for your birthday girl or boy is not only easy, it's a clever way to get your preschoolers moving—without them catching on to the act. Remember: Preschoolers' attention only lasts a few minutes at a time, so don't worry if you have to jump from activity to activity.

■ **WALK THE TIGHT ROPE:** Lay a jump rope or bungee cord on the ground and have the "tight-rope walkers" walk back and forth while balancing on the rope. It's a challenge even flat on the ground!

■ **JUGGLE:** Give two of your guests a mini soccer ball or soft, big ball. Have them stand a few feet away from each other and toss the ball back and forth. Add a second ball into the mix to imitate a juggler.

■ **HULA HOOP ACROBAT:** Place two hula hoops flat on the ground and have the kids jump in and out of the hoops and from hoop to hoop. Ask them to put their arms through mini hula hoops, with their arms straight out to their sides. Have them make big circles with their arms, so the hoops keep moving.

■ **BATON TWIRL:** March to a jaunty tune while the birthday girl or boy leads the way, pumping a baton up and down.

■ **MAKE LIKE A SEAL:** Take a large feather and challenge your "seals" to keep it in the air by blowing on it from below. Then have them balance a plastic plate on their heads for as long as they can. Extra bonus: Ask them to walk back and forth while balancing the plate.

■ **BE A RINGMASTER:** Hand the baton to your guests so they can "train" stuffed animals. Encourage them to wave the baton and to "show" the animals how to jump and roar.

■ **"FEETS" OF BICYCLE DARING:** Have them lie on their backs, raise their feet in the air, and cycle their legs.

■ **"FLAMING" BATONS:** Take some scarves (preferably red or orange) and have them toss them in the air and catch them.

■ **TUMBLING CLOWNS:** Show your stars how to do a forward roll: have them place their hands on the ground in front of them, tuck their chin to their chest, and roll forward (with Mom or Dad spotting).

BONUS: Break out the face paint to help your clowns get into a goofy mood. Or, if it's easier, a little dab of lipstick on their noses and cheeks will do the trick.

Excuse Buster!

How do I respond when my little slugs put up a fight in the face of exercise?

Getting preschoolers motivated is all about fun and distraction. You'll be surprised how quickly they'll become motivated if they see they can have more fun by participating than by pouting—especially if they see other kids having a ball in front of them, so consider recruiting a playmate or older sibling. Preschoolers are also easily distracted, so you can get them involved by directing their focus little by little to the activity. For example: "Wow! I think I just saw the most beautiful butterfly ever! What colors can butterflies be? Come help me see if we can catch some butterflies."

#6: The Big Bailout

This is one of Larysa's daughter Bella's favorite warm-weather activities. She uses her favorite elephant watering can, but a bucket will do just as well.

What you'll need: A baby pool, a bucket

Who's playing: Preschoolers

How many: 1 or more

Prime time: Sunny Days

Fill a baby pool with water and challenge your little swimmer to scoop out the water with a bucket, dumping it in the flowerbeds or lawn.

FITNESS FACTOR: Strength, Cardio, Flexibility

COVERT CALORIES: She'll burn 50 calories in 30 minutes.

SNEAKY SUPERCHARGE: Give her a smaller bucket, which will require her to make more trips.

SAFETY PRECAUTIONS: Keep a careful eye on your child any time she's near water. Even a small amount of water can pose a drowning hazard.

#7: Bubble Bobble

Larysa's Nicholas means business when it comes to bubbles—he uses a ping-pong paddle to pop them.

What you'll need: A bottle of bubbles

Who's playing: Preschoolers

How many: 1 or more

Prime time: Sunny Days

Blow bubbles—then challenge your kids to run and catch them. (Optional: Arm the kids with ping-pong paddles or Wiffle ball bats to pop the bubbles.)

FITNESS FACTOR: Cardio, Mood Booster!

COVERT CALORIES: Pop 109 calories in just 30 minutes.

SNEAKY SUPERCHARGE: Time them to see how fast they can pop the bubbles.

#8: Wave Tag

On a trip to the Oregon coast, the Lapines stood at the ocean's edge and dared the cold waves to touch their toes—only to run back up the beach to dry sand each time the waves rolled in. The fun was in getting as close as possible without getting their feet wet.

What you'll need: The beach!

Who's playing: Preschoolers, Grade-Schoolers

How many: 1 or more

Prime time: Sunny Days, Weekends

Play wave tag: When a wave comes in, have your child run in the opposite direction then tease it by following it back to the ocean.

FITNESS FACTOR: Cardio, Strength, Mood Booster!

COVERT CALORIES: She'll burn 109 calories in 30 minutes.

SNEAKY SUPERCHARGE: Add balance and coordination by having her try to jump over the low waves when they come in, which will burn 136 calories every half hour.

SAFETY PRECAUTIONS: As always, when your child is playing near the water, keep a careful eye on her.

Good Morning Workout

It's not always easy to greet the day with energy, even for little kids. That's why Larysa likes to start her morning doing a few of these stretches with her kids soon after they wake up—it gets the blood moving and gives them a little quiet time before their busy days. Do each stretch for about a minute or two. If you have time, rotate through the "menagerie" twice. They'll never know they're doing yoga, one of the best workouts of all.

■ **BUTTERFLY FLIGHT:** Have your child sit on his tush with the soles of his feet pressed against each other and his knees out to the side. Ask him to flap his knees up and down mimicking a butterfly's flight.

■ **SNAKE DANCE:** Ask her to stretch out on the ground on her belly and place her hands by her ears. Show her how to push her upper body up, like a cobra raising its head, leaving her hips and lower body on the floor. Tell her to give a big hissssss like a snake.

■ **KING KONG:** Have him stand up and raise each arm, alternately, to the sky, pretending to grab bananas from a tree. Then beat on his chest and yell, "Ooh, Ooh, Ooh!" like an ape.

■ **CRAZY CAT:** Ask her to get down on all fours and gently roll her back into an arched position. Flatten the back and return to an arched position. Repeat. Finish with a big, "Mee-owww!"

■ **FROG ON A LILY PAD:** Show him how to stand with his feet shoulder-width apart, toes pointed out. Have him bend his knees over his toes, lift his heels off the ground, and put his hands on the floor. Let out a "Riiiibiiit!"

■ **BARKING DOG:** Ask her to get on all fours. Have her slowly straighten her legs and stick her tush in the air. Lean back, straightening her arms. See who can "woof" the loudest.

#9: Huff and Puff

This activity involves some parental participation, giving the whole family a workout.

What you'll need: A *Three Little Pigs* storybook

Who's playing: Preschoolers

How many: 1 or more

Prime time: Any Day, Rainy Days, Weekends

Act out the story of the Three Little Pigs. Take the role of the Big, Bad Wolf and chase your squealing piglets around the house or the yard.

• • • • •

FITNESS FACTOR: Cardio, Mood Booster!

COVERT CALORIES: They'll burn 54 calories every half hour.

SNEAKY SUPERCHARGE: Have them build a "house" out of sheets and couch cushions. After the Big, Bad Wolf blows it down, have them rebuild it, which will add strength, balance, and flexibility.

The Preschooler Playlist

Albums that will have their little toes tapping:

1. Laurie Berkner, *Rocketship Run*
2. The Wiggles, *Getting Strong CD*
3. Uncle Moondog, *Uncle Moondog*
4. Drew's Famous, *Kid's Silly Songs*
5. Sesame Street, *Hot! Hot! Hot! Dance Songs*

#10: Sock Hop!

Did you know socks can deliver a whopping of a hopping? Here's a fun way to approach exercise and laundry. Your kids may be so anxious to get to the fun part of this activity that they may forget to match their socks properly.

What you'll need: A clean load of socks

Who's playing: Preschoolers, Grade-Schoolers

How many: 1 or more

Prime time: Any Day, Rainy Days

Challenge your child to match all the clean socks in a load of laundry. Then see if she can toss them into the basket.

FITNESS FACTOR: Cardio, Coordination

COVERT CALORIES: Your child will burn more than a calorie per minute.

SNEAKY SUPERCHARGE: Put the laundry basket farther and farther away after each sock lands. Or, have your child stand across the room and toss the sock to her ("1, 2, 3, hike!") and have her run to put the socks in the drawer, which will add some strength and even more coordination.

Quick Tip!

Save time *and* save energy. Missy waits until she's got a full load before washing laundry, since it takes just as much energy to do a small load as it does a big one.

Fun fact! According to the California Energy Commission, American families do about 400 loads of laundry a year. That's 400 chances to sneak some exercise in!

#11: Get Me to the ER—STAT!

Bella loves playing "animal" ER. Her favorite "patients" are her two pet schnauzers. She chases them around the house, "rescues" them, and rushes them to her "veterinary hospital" that is set up in the living room. If you don't have four-legged playmates, a stuffed animal will fill in just as well.

What you'll need: A favorite stuffed animal, bandages, a toy stroller (optional)

Who's playing: Preschoolers, Grade-Schoolers

How many: 1 or more

Prime time: Any Day, Rainy Days, Playdates

Play "ambulance." Have your child run to find her "injured" animal or doll. Put her favorite friend in the toy stroller and race back to the "veterinary hospital" in another room where she can apply bandages. Once the toy is on the mend, have her bring it back for some well-deserved rest.

FITNESS FACTOR: Cardio, Coordination

COVERT CALORIES: She'll burn 34 calories in 30 minutes.

SNEAKY SUPERCHARGE: Take the "injured" animal to a special hospital via "helicopter," which requires a few more laps around the house.

#12: Van "Go"

Creating art doesn't have to be a static activity. Painters in the style of "The Sneaky Fitness School" know that artwork and movement can go hand in hand.

What you'll need: An easel, markers, crayons, chalk and/or paint

Who's playing: Preschoolers, Grade-Schoolers

How many: 1

Prime time: Any Day, Rainy Days

Instead of setting up your budding artist to paint at a table, put up a double-sided easel. Encourage him to walk from one side of the easel to the other, by having him use chalk on one side and markers or paint on the other.

FITNESS FACTOR: Cardio, Strength, Coordination

COVERT CALORIES: Painting while standing burns 14 more calories in 30 minutes than sitting.

SNEAKY SUPERCHARGE: Time her to see how fast she can replicate the picture she drew on one side on the other side, which will add another 7 more calories per half hour of vigorous painting.

#13: Muscle Murals

Why worry about coloring in the lines when you have a huge piece of paper to fill? Larysa's kids especially love when she supercharges the fun by painting murals with their feet. They howl with laughter when she pretends she doesn't remember she has paint on her feet and "starts" to step off the paper and on the floor.

What you'll need: Mural paper (available at any craft store), finger paint, crayons, markers, or chalk

Who's playing: Preschoolers, Grade-Schoolers

How many: 1 or more

Prime time: Any Day, Rainy Days, Weekends, Playdates

Roll a long piece of mural paper on the floor and let her paint or color up and down the room.

FITNESS FACTOR: Flexibility, Cardio, Balance

COVERT CALORIES: She'll burn 41 calories in 30 minutes.

SNEAKY SUPERCHARGE: Add a bit more coordination to the day by having her paint with her toes! Place an old drop cloth, towel, or bathmat alongside the paper to catch the mess. Set out paper plates covered with a thin layer of finger paint for her to step on, and a plastic container of water to rinse off her feet when she wants to switch hues.

#14: Set Up Shop

Playing store is a game that we loved when we were little, and our kids enjoy now too. Only one thing has changed since we were their age: We now know that it's fun and good for you!

What you'll need: A pantry

Who's playing: Preschoolers, Grade-Schoolers

How many: 1 or more

Prime time: Rainy Days, Playdates

Let your kids raid your pantry for cans to set up on the countertop as a store. Let them lift, carry, stack, and arrange the goods. When it comes time for the "customers" to pay, have them bag the groceries and help carry them to the "car."

FITNESS FACTOR: Strength, Cardio

COVERT CALORIES: Your store clerks will burn 48 calories in 30 minutes.

SNEAKY SUPERCHARGE: Leave the 16-ounce cans out of reach and stock up on the 20-ounce ones instead.

#15: Big Foot

You've always wanted your kids to follow in your footsteps! Here's a way to do just that while helping to keep their hearts healthy and muscles strong. (P.S. This activity also works on the beach—without the boots, of course!)

What you'll need: A pair of snow boots

Who's playing: Preschoolers, Grade-Schoolers

How many: 1 or more

Prime time: Snowy Days, Weekends

Make footprints in the snow and challenge your child to step from footprint to footprint.

• • • • •

FITNESS FACTOR: Cardio, Balance, Strength, Coordination, Mood Booster!

COVERT CALORIES: She'll burn 109 calories in 30 minutes.

SNEAKY SUPERCHARGE: Lengthen your stride so she has to jump from print to print. Or, lead her up a hill or two, which doubles the amount of calories she'll expend.

Sneaky Tip!

Don't stay cooped up when there's snow on the ground—anything you can do to get your kids out playing in the snow is good exercise, as it takes a lot of exertion to walk in it—particularly if you've got on boots. So bundle him up for some wintery activities!

#16: Graffiti Artist

Behold the power of the spray bottle! Our kids won't come inside until the very last squirt.

What you'll need: Plastic spray bottles, food coloring

Who's playing: Preschoolers, Grade-Schoolers

How many: 1 or more

Prime time: Snowy Days, Playdates, Weekends

Fill a few spray bottles with water and food coloring, and let him "spray paint" a mural on your snow-covered lawn.

FITNESS FACTOR: Balance, Cardio, Mood Booster!

COVERT CALORIES: Taking it to the snow will burn twice as many calories as painting a mural indoors.

SNEAKY SUPERCHARGE: Paint a hopscotch board in the snow and have him hop his way through the snow—it'll triple the amount of calories he'll burn and add coordination and strength.

#17: Snow Roll

Larysa's kids build a snowball that they add to with each storm until it gets too big to move—or until it melts.

What you'll need: Hats, mittens, scarves

Who's playing: Preschoolers, Grade-Schoolers

How many: 2 or more

Prime time: Snow Days, Playdates, Weekends

Challenge your kids to see who can roll the biggest snowball.

FITNESS FACTOR: Strength, Cardio, Mood Booster!

COVERT CALORIES: They'll burn 114 calories for every hour they're outside.

SNEAKY SUPERCHARGE: Double the calories by having them race with their snowballs. Or, have them roll the snowball up a hill, push it down, and then back up.

#18: Rain on Your Parade

Don't let a cloudy day keep your kids from getting outside. Have them pull on some fun, colored boots and give the day a bright boost!

What you'll need: Rain boots, rain coat

Who's playing: Preschoolers, Grade-Schoolers

How many: 1 or more

Prime time: Rainy Days

Take a walk, jumping from one puddle to the next.

FITNESS FACTOR: Cardio, Balance, Mood Booster!

COVERT CALORIES: This burns 37 calories every 10 minutes.

SNEAKY SUPERCHARGE: Play Red Light, Green Light in the rain. The rain makes it a little muddy and slippery and so much more fun (and more active because kids have to work to stop themselves).

SAFETY PRECAUTION: Keep an eye on your puddle jumpers when they're slipping and sliding to make sure they're not playing in an area where a slip can mean them falling on top of something hard—or sliding into the street.

#19: Volatile Volcano

Running through the sprinklers never gets old. Be forewarned: you may want to jump in, too!

What you'll need: A lawn sprinkler, set to intermittent (or a Mount Tiki Soki®).

Who's playing: Preschoolers, Grade-Schoolers

How many: 1 or more

Prime time: Sunny Days, Playdates, Weekends

Set up the sprinkler and let them go—have them jump through the water stream, jump over the water as it squirts, and try to run away from it before it "catches" them.

FITNESS FACTOR: Cardio, Coordination, Strength, Mood Booster!

COVERT CALORIES: At 245 calories per hour, this is a real crowd pleaser.

SNEAKY SUPERCHARGE: If a child gets squirted she must freeze until another child touches her.

#20: Night Lights

Nothing announces summer better than the arrival of lightning bugs.

What you'll need: A clear plastic container with air holes punched in the top

Who's playing: Preschoolers, Grade-Schoolers

How many: 1 or more

Prime time: Summer evenings

Have your kids run to catch fireflies. See who can collect the most. The next morning, let them go!

FITNESS FACTOR: Cardio, Mood Booster!

COVERT CALORIES: Your evening adventurers will burn 109 calories every half hour.

SNEAKY SUPERCHARGE: Time them to see who can catch the most bugs in 30 minutes.

Fun fact! Fireflies are efficient! 100 percent of their glow is given off as light, not heat. In comparison, a typical light bulb gives off 10 percent light and 90 percent wasted heat.

#21: Sidewalk Art

Tap into their artistic vision—without worrying about them making a mess.

What you'll need: A bucket, paint brushes, water

Who's playing: Preschoolers, Grade-Schoolers

How many: 1 or more

Prime time: Sunny Days, Playdates, Weekends

Hand them a bucket of water and let them "paint" the sidewalk, driveway, or even the outside of the house with it.

FITNESS FACTOR: Cardio, Flexibility, Coordination

COVERT CALORIES: Your street artists will burn 48 calories in a half hour.

SNEAKY SUPERCHARGE: Dump out the excess water and let them splash around in the puddles, which will add 54 calories in 15 minutes.

#22: Look Ma, No Feet!

*Sometimes all it takes to get kids moving is to tell them they **can't** do something.*

What you'll need: Willing children

Who's playing: Preschoolers, Grade-Schoolers

How many: 1 or more

Prime time: Any Day

Tell your kids that they can't *walk* to their room, but have to *slither* like a snake.

FITNESS FACTOR: Cardio, Strength, Flexibility, Coordination

COVERT CALORIES: For every 15 minutes they slither, they'll burn 24 calories.

SNEAKY SUPERCHARGE: Challenge them to a "Betcha Can't" Contest. For example, tell them: "Betcha can't hop like a frog across the kitchen or crab-walk to the bedroom."

#23: Noah's Ark

You don't need to have them line up two-by-two, but this is a fun way to see how many different animal walks your kids can come up with. It looks like so much fun that the neighborhood kids always get in on it (as do the parents).

What you'll need: A few of your kid's friends

Who's playing: Preschoolers, Grade-Schoolers

How many: 2 or more

Prime time: Sunny Days, Playdates, Parties

Hold a race, asking your kids and their friends to run like different animals—frogs, ducks, bunnies, kangaroos, crabs (who run sideways), shrimp (who run backward on all fours), etc.

FITNESS FACTOR: Cardio, Balance, Flexibility, Coordination, Mood Booster!

COVERT CALORIES: They'll burn 68 calories in a half hour.

SNEAKY SUPERCHARGE: Have them play leap frog as they race from one end of the yard to another.

#24: Fireman Drill

Firemen need to get into their gear quickly. This activity may even help speed your morning routine along—no alarm bells necessary.

What you'll need: Your child's clothes for the day

Who's playing: Preschoolers, Grade-schoolers

How many: 1 or more

Prime time: Any Day

Challenge your child to beat the clock as she gets dressed, just like firemen do. (It may help younger kids to lay out the clothes for them.)

FITNESS FACTOR: Cardio, Flexibility, Balance, Coordination

COVERT CALORIES: She'll burn about a calorie a minute.

SNEAKY SUPERCHARGE: Place a list of clothing items on the wall and have your child run to check off the item that she's put on after each addition.

#25: How Many?

Larysa's husband, Steven, loves playing this game with the kids, which keeps them moving and helps them count. To challenge them even more, he asks them to count in Ukrainian and Spanish as well as English.

What you'll need: Your imagination

Who's playing: Preschoolers, Grade-Schoolers

How many: 1 or more

Prime time: Any Day

Ask your child to find out how many skips, jumps, and hops it would take to get from one place to another. For example, how many skips would it take to get from the car to the house?

FITNESS FACTOR: Cardio, Balance, Coordination, Mood Booster!

COVERT CALORIES: They'll burn 73 calories in 20 minutes.

SNEAKY SUPERCHARGE: Time him to see how many seconds it would take him to sprint from one place to another.

#26: Project Runway

Missy's girls dress up in her and Rick's clothes, but the rule is they have to hang each outfit back on the hanger before donning the next one, which is a lot of work. Younger kids, like Bella and her friends, love having fashion shows for their stuffed animals—the animals are the paparazzi, and the girls strut and pose for them. The girls can do this for hours, going back and forth between closets and "runways" burning calories as they march, reach to hang items back up and wiggle in and out of the clothes.

What you'll need: Dress-up clothes

Who's playing: Preschoolers, Grade-Schoolers

How many: 1 or more

Prime time: Any Day, Rainy Days, Playdates

Let your kid dress up and model different outfits and then walk back and forth on the "runway," located down the hall or on a separate floor from the closets. Put on some music to help her strut her stuff.

FITNESS FACTOR: Cardio, Flexibility, Balance, Coordination

COVERT CALORIES: Your fashionistas will burn 54 calories in an hour.

SNEAKY SUPERCHARGE: Give her some of your clothes to wear—they're heavier and harder to get in and out of so it will burn more calories.

#27: Ice, Ice Baby

Forget the etiquette school lesson of balancing a book on your head—our version is way "cooler," while still teaching grace and balance. We tried this many times with Bella and Sammy and their giggles alone were worth the effort!

What you'll need: One ice cube per child

Who's playing: Preschoolers, Grade-Schoolers, Tweens

How many: 1 or more

Prime time: Any Day, Summer Days, Playdates

Challenge your child to balance an ice cube on his head. See how far he can walk without it falling.

● ● ● ● ●

FITNESS FACTOR: Balance, Strength

COVERT CALORIES: He'll burn 9 calories in 10 minutes' time.

SNEAKY SUPERCHARGE: See if he can squat without the ice cube sliding off.

Quick Tip!

Thinking about getting your child a two-wheeler? Consider this: a BMX® bike burns more than twice the amount of calories as a regular leisure bike and requires a good deal more balance, coordination, strength and cardio to ride it. Littler kids may benefit from a Big Wheels® over a tricycle, too, since those have little leverage and the kids have to pedal extra hard.

#28: Getta Load of This!

Kids are really good at creating a lot of laundry, but they can also be good at helping you do the laundry as well. Little do they know that in doing so, they're also helping themselves get strong and fit!

What you'll need: Whatever is in your hamper!

Who's playing: Preschoolers, Grade-Schoolers and, if you're lucky, the occasional Tween

How many: 1 or more

Prime time: Any day (or anytime you've got a load of laundry going, which, let's face it, is always).

Ask your child to help you put the laundry away, but only give her a few items at a time, so she'll have to go up and down and all around the house.

FITNESS FACTOR: Cardio, Strength

COVERT CALORIES: In just 20 minutes, she'll burn 50 extra calories.

SNEAKY SUPERCHARGE: Time her to see how fast she can get back and forth delivering her clean load. And don't forget to see how fast she can scoop up the dirty laundry to take back to the machines after she's done. Running burns twice as many calories as walking.

#29: Paint the Town Red (or Blue or Green)

Missy's daughter Emily truly thinks outside the box—she prefers her artwork to be interactive.

What you'll need: Sidewalk chalk

Who's playing: Preschoolers, Grade-Schoolers, Tweens

How many: 1 or more

Prime time: Sunny Days, Weekends, Playdates

Quick Tip!

Short on time? Put a piece of chalk in your child's hand and let her run around in large circles to draw a spiral on the driveway. The faster she goes, the more giggles you'll hear!

Set your artist loose on the driveway or sidewalk with some colored chalk and her imagination. Have her draw a huge mural or a city, town, park, or castle—making the map as big as she can.

• • • • •

FITNESS FACTOR: Flexibility, Cardio, Mood Booster!

COVERT CALORIES: Your graffiti artist will burn 50 calories in 30 minutes.

SNEAKY SUPERCHARGE: She built it, now she can enjoy it. Have her ride her bike or run from place to place, burning an additional 54 calories—as she pretends to stop off at the town market, take a tour, or jump over her castle's moat. Let her imagination be her guide!

#30: Waitress Workout

Most kids we know are in charge of helping to set and clear the table. If they're already doing it, why not give it a healthy twist?

What you'll need: Your regular dinner plates, cups, napkins, and silverware

Who's playing: Preschoolers, Grade-Schoolers, Tweens

How many: 1 or more

Prime time: Any Day

Ask your child to set and clear the table—but only let him take one thing back and forth at a time. Tell him it's not polite to stack dishes at the table (true fact!).

FITNESS FACTOR: Cardio

COVERT CALORIES: How's this for a tip: They'll burn 20 calories in 15 minutes.

SNEAKY SUPERCHARGE: Time him to see how fast he can do it. Or, see if he can balance paper or plastic plates (clean, empty ones!) on his head from the kitchen to the table, which adds a bit of balance and coordination.

SAFETY PRECAUTIONS: Make sure your little ones are only carrying plastic cups and plates, and leave the forks and knives to the adults or older kids.

#31: Wobble Hobble

Our kids love field day activities like egg-and-spoon races and water balloon tosses. Here's a game that combines both.

What you'll need: One water balloon for each child

Who's playing: Preschoolers, Grade-Schoolers, Tweens

How many: 2 or more

Prime time: Sunny Days, Playdates, Parties

Have your child place a water balloon between his knees and race to the finish line without dropping it. After the races, have her put a water balloon down her shirt, tuck it in, and jump up and down to make it jiggle until it drops or pops.

FITNESS FACTOR: Cardio, Coordination, Balance, Mood Booster!

COVERT CALORIES: She'll burn 68 calories in 15 minutes.

SNEAKY SUPERCHARGE: Instead of walking or running, have your child jump to the finish line, which will add 54 more calories to the tally. Or make a rule that if she drops the balloon before getting to the end, she has to start all over again.

SAFETY PRECAUTIONS: Be sure to pick up and throw out any pieces of the popped balloon as they can be a choking hazard to young children and animals.

#32: Halo Optional

Bella loves to make a "choir" of snow angels. When she's done, she jumps up and pretends to be the conductor!

What you'll need: Mittens, hats, scarves

Who's playing: Preschoolers, Grade-Schoolers, Tweens

How many: 1 or more

Prime time: Snowy Days, Playdates

Challenge your kids to cover your yard in snow angels.

• • • • •

FITNESS FACTOR: Balance, Flexibility, Cardio, Coordination, Strength, Mood Booster!

COVERT CALORIES: They'll burn 86 calories in an hour.

SNEAKY SUPERCHARGE: Help your child build and conduct a snow angel symphony.

Quick Tip!

The Sneaky Chef reminds parents to keep portions under control by using salad or smaller plates instead of dinner plates—your kids will think they're getting more of a heaping helping than they actually are. Don't just hand them the bag of chips, either. Instead, serve snacks in small bowls so your kids aren't tempted to keep dipping in. (These methods work for moms too!)

#33: Fit Fort

Whether their imagination takes them to a medieval castle, a foxhole, or the Alamo, building a snow fort will keep your little soldiers in shape.

What you'll need: A sand bucket and some snow

Who's playing: Preschoolers, Grade-Schoolers, Tweens

How many: 1 or more

Prime time: Snowy Days, Playdates, Weekends

Show your kids how to build a snow fort by using sand buckets to pack the snow and stack the shapes like an igloo.

FITNESS FACTOR: Strength, Cardio, Mood Booster!

COVERT CALORIES: They'll burn 114 calories in an hour.

SNEAKY SUPERCHARGE: Add some furniture to the fort—build chairs, tables, and fridges from the snow.

#34: Lawn Limbo

Who doesn't like letting loose on the lawn with a bathing suit on a hot day?

What you'll need: A hose with a spray nozzle

Who's playing: Preschoolers, Grade-Schoolers, Tweens

How many: 1 or 1more

Prime time: Sunny Days, Playdates, Weekends

Squirt a hose in a steady, horizontal stream starting at your shoulder height and have your kids limbo underneath the water. Lower the hose after each kid gets a turn.

FITNESS FACTOR: Cardio, Flexibility, Mood Booster!

COVERT CALORIES: This activity burns a cool 109 calories per hour.

SNEAKY SUPERCHARGE: Challenge the kids to jump over the horizontal stream, which will add strength and 136 calories in just a half hour.

#35: Freeze Dance

When the DiDios play, they keep all kinds of music on the playlist—country, polka, Latin, and even opera!

What you'll need: An iPod, CD-player, or radio

Who's playing: Preschoolers, Grade-Schoolers, Tweens

How many: 1 or more

Prime time: Any Day, Playdates, Parties

Be the DJ. (Or, if you've got more than one kid playing, take turns letting the kids "spin.") Tell them to dance until the DJ stops the music. They have to stand absolutely still in whatever funny pose they're in until the DJ starts the music again.

• • • • •

FITNESS FACTOR: Cardio, Balance, Coordination, Flexibility, Mood Booster!

COVERT CALORIES: Boogie your way to burning about 60 calories in 30 minutes.

SNEAKY SUPERCHARGE: Have them sit and freeze when the music stops, which helps build strength.

Grade-Schooler Playlist

Albums that will make your grade-schooler want to boogie:

1. Fisher Price Rockin' Dance Party
2. Drew's Famous, *Family Fun*
3. Radio Disney, *Jams Vol. 9*
4. More Kidz Bop Gold
5. Drew's Famous, *Kids Go Wild*

#36: Lost Toy Treasure Hunt

If your house is like ours, your kids' toys seem to have a life of their own. Pieces of puzzles and games and tiny toy parts go astray. Collect them all and watch your kids get a workout—that's a lot of hidden treasure!

What you'll need: Flashlights, a laundry basket

Who's playing: Preschoolers, Grade-Schoolers, Tweens

How many: 1 or more

Prime time: Any Day, Rainy Days

Hand out flashlights and let the kids crawl under beds and couches, lift up pillows, peer into closets, search through boxes, and reach into nooks and crannies—anywhere a lost toy can be. Keep a laundry basket in a central location for your Lost Toy Hunters to deposit their finds. Encourage them to go up and down stairs, back and forth, throughout the house.

FITNESS FACTOR: Cardio, Flexibility, Strength

COVERT CALORIES: They'll burn 41 calories every 30 minutes.

SNEAKY SUPERCHARGE: Challenge them to crawl from room to room.

#37: Power Hour

Surprise your kids by declaring a spontaneous "theme" hour. It's silly enough that they'll be too entertained to realize they're getting a secret dose of exercise.

What you'll need: A little ingenuity

Who's playing: Preschoolers, Grade-Schoolers, Tweens

How many: 1 or more

Prime time: Weekends

Declare that for the next hour, kids have to dance, hop, and skip wherever they are going.

FITNESS FACTOR: Cardio, Balance, Coordination, Mood Booster!

COVERT CALORIES: They'll burn up to three times the amount of calories they otherwise would that hour.

SNEAKY SUPERCHARGE: Do it in double time, which will burn even more calories.

#38: Mountaineers

This may be the easiest way for anyone of any age to fit more fitness into their daily life: Turn your back on taking elevators or escalators and aim for the stairwell instead. Larysa's kids think that elevators never work properly because she's always telling them they're broken before steering them to the stairs.

What you'll need: A staircase

Who's playing: Preschoolers, Grade-Schoolers, Tweens

How many: 1 or more

Prime time: Any Day

Next time you find yourself at the bottom of a staircase, pretend that you and your child are mountaineers. Point to the top and say it's the peak of Mount Everest, where the best and bravest explorers in the world have reached, and see how high she can go. With younger kids, you can count out loud the number of stairs she tackles as she goes. (For preschoolers, one to two flights of stairs should be sufficient, but don't discourage them if they want to try for one or two more.)

FITNESS FACTOR: Cardio, Strength, Mood Booster!

COVERT CALORIES: They'll burn 36 calories every 10 minutes they climb.

SNEAKY SUPERCHARGE: Show her how to take steps two at a time, go up two steps and down one, or step up leading with her left foot twice, then her right foot twice, all of which will make her work just a little harder. Hold the rail for safety!

#39: Little Miss Crabby

Just like walking in snow, walking in sand makes you work just that much harder, burning more calories as you go. Bella and Nicholas love finding shells and sandcrabs on Maryland beaches. They'll spend all day digging for these natural treasures.

What you'll need: A sand bucket, shovel (optional)

Who's playing: Preschoolers, Grade-Schoolers, Tweens

How many: 1 or more

Prime time: Sunny Days, Weekends

Challenge your child to see how many shells she can find by digging through the wet sand at the shoreline.

FITNESS FACTOR: Strength, Cardio, Flexibility, Balance, Mood Booster!

COVERT CALORIES: She'll burn 109 calories every hour.

SNEAKY SUPERCHARGE: Have her imitate a crab by doing a crabwalk back to the towel, which will help build coordination.

SAFETY PRECAUTIONS: As always, keep a close eye on your children when they are playing near water.

Playground Mania

By now your kids are probably familiar faces at the playground. But why should a trip to the playground be old hat? Rev up their playtime by adding a little fun, competitive fitness. While exercises may vary depending on the equipment that's available at your playground, the ideas here are examples that can inspire you. Time your child to see how fast she can do the following, but be sure to promote competitiveness with her own times, instead of having her race against someone else. Rotate through them quickly. Do it three times and see what her best time is.

- 10 jumping jacks
- Side step to monkey bars
- Pull herself across monkey bars
- Hop on one foot on mini trampoline
- Do 10 jumps of trampoline
- Gallop to swings
- Run across a bridge/through a tire path
- Hop on other foot to rock wall/rope ladder
- Go up rock wall/rope ladder, down slide, and tag a home base, such as a bench.

#40: Pound Puppy

Your kids have been begging for one and now they're old enough to truly take care of it. Get them the dog they've always wanted. Sure, it will teach them responsibility, but it will also get them moving. Missy's girls play this game with Princess, their Labrador retriever, in the snow using snowballs instead of tennis balls. (Larysa once suggested a client get a dog for her inactive son. She got a pug, and her son got more exercise than he bargained for, since he had to carry the dog everywhere!)

What you'll need: Your favorite pooch, a tennis ball

Who's playing: Preschoolers, Grade-Schoolers, Tweens

How many: 1 or more

Prime time: Any Day, Sunny Days

Walking, bathing, and caring for a dog takes a lot of energy. Give a game of fetch a sneaky boost by having your child throw the ball and run to see who can get to it first—her or Fido.

● ● ● ● ●

FITNESS FACTOR: Cardio, Coordination, Mood Booster!

COVERT CALORIES: Your child will burn 218 calories for every hour with her pooch.

SNEAKY SUPERCHARGE: Get two dogs! (Larysa did!) Or, keep both your kids and dogs interested in playing longer by offering different items for the dog to fetch, such as various-sized balls, stuffed animals, rubber toys, etc.

Fun fact! Not all dogs are created equal. Some require more energy than others. Topping the perky pooch list are Beagles, Border Collies, Weimaraners, Greyhounds, and Jack Russell terriers.

#41: Walk This Way

Day trips to water parks, theme parks, zoos, and other recreation sites are the perfect decoy for fitting in fitness—after all, there are plenty of opportunities to stay on your feet and lots of ground to cover.

What you'll need: A fun destination

Who's playing: Preschoolers, Grade-Schoolers, Tweens (if you're lucky)

How many: 1 or more

Prime time: Sunny Days, Rainy Days, Weekends

Touring around a zoo, theme park, or science museum can burn a lot of calories if you act a bit uncivilized. Don't just have your kids walk from exhibit to exhibit. Instead, have them imitate the animals, characters, or theme they've just seen as they go—lope like a lion, march like a soldier, strut like a mummy.

FITNESS FACTOR: Cardio, Mood Booster!

COVERT CALORIES: Three hours of park-time will burn 204 calories.

SNEAKY SUPERCHARGE: Don't follow the map—visit sites on opposite ends of the park and back again.

SAFETY PRECAUTIONS: Make sure your kids are well hydrated and have on comfy clothes, shoes, and sunscreen—or your day will be cut too short because of burns and blisters.

#42: Pop! Pop!

It can't get easier—or more inexpensive—than this, once again proving our theory that kids sometimes prefer the package's wrapping to what's inside.

What you'll need: Bubble wrap, either purchased at an office-supply store or repurposed from a package

Who's playing: Preschoolers, Grade-Schoolers, Tweens

How many: 1 or more

Prime time: Any Day, Rainy Days

Spread the bubble wrap on the floor and let her jump on it until all the bubbles are popped.

FITNESS FACTOR: Cardio, Mood Booster!

COVERT CALORIES: 20 minutes of popping will burn 91 calories.

SNEAKY SUPERCHARGE: Challenge her to hop on one foot, which helps improve balance.

SAFETY PRECAUTIONS: Keep an eye on very small children when there are plastic bags and sheets around, as they can pose a suffocation hazard.

#43: Get Down, Get Clean

Sure, Cinderella had some magic mice to help her with the housework. The magic here is that your kids will be getting a workout while they work.

What you'll need: A stereo, iPod, or CD player

Who's playing: Preschoolers, Grade-Schoolers, Tweens

How many: 1 or more

Prime time: Any Day

Watch your children flex their muscles *and* clean their room—turn on the tunes and challenge them to finish cleaning their rooms before the song ends.

FITNESS FACTOR: Cardio, Strength, Balance, Flexibility, Coordination

COVERT CALORIES: They'll burn 48 calories every half hour.

SNEAKY SUPERCHARGE: Let them jump on the bed after every chore (before making it, of course!); it will burn 16 more calories and help with their core strength.

#44: Temper Tantrum

You may think we're crazy when we suggest your child throw a tantrum, but it will not only help her blow off some steam—she'll burn some calories, too.

What you'll need: A pillow, newspapers

Who's playing: Preschoolers, Grade-Schoolers, Tweens

How many: 1 or more

Prime time: Any Day

Have an angry kid on your hands? Show her how to let off some steam by stomping her feet, ripping up old newspapers, or kicking a pillow. Chances are she'll start laughing so hard she'll forget why she was mad in the first place.

FITNESS FACTOR: Cardio, Strength, Coordination, Mood Booster!

COVERT CALORIES: In 15 minutes, she'll burn 68 calories. (We hope the tantrum doesn't last longer than that!)

SNEAKY SUPERCHARGE: When you've got their attention, tell them to "run off their steam" by doing laps around the house, which will burn 36 calories in 10 minutes.

#45: Twinkle Toes

*Almost as amusing as Tom Hanks dancing on a giant piano in the movie **Big**, this activity will elicit a lot of giggles and some interesting tunes.*

What you'll need: A piano or keyboard (toy or otherwise)

Who's playing: Preschoolers, Grade-Schoolers, Tweens

How many: 1

Prime time: Any Day, Rainy Days

Put the keyboard or toy piano on the floor, then have your little Mozart sit in front of it (on the ground or in a chair), and challenge him to play a tune with his toes!

FITNESS FACTOR: Cardio, Balance, Coordination, Mood Booster!

COVERT CALORIES: He'll burn 23 calories every 20 minutes.

SNEAKY SUPERCHARGE: Have him play with his elbows and nose—it'll extend the fun and increase core strength and coordination.

#46: Roll with It

All you need is a little hill to make a big impact on your kid's health.

What you'll need: A hill

Who's playing: Preschoolers, Grade-Schoolers, Tweens

How many: 1 or more

Prime time: Sunny Days

Show your kids how to roll down a hill, and walk back up again.

FITNESS FACTOR: Cardio, Flexibility, Balance, Strength, Mood Booster!

COVERT CALORIES: She'll burn 82 calories in 60 minutes.

SNEAKY SUPERCHARGE: Challenge your kid to climb back up the hill in various ways: sprint, gallop, skip and side step, which will double how many calories she burns.

#47: See You Later Alligator

Whether your little adventurer is pretending she's in the Amazon or the Everglades, let her imagination run wild. (This is a great game to play during commercial breaks!)

What you'll need: Your furniture

Who's playing: Preschoolers, Grade-Schoolers, Tweens

How many: 1 or more

Prime time: Any Day, Rainy Days

Have your child pretend there are alligators on the floor of the room and have him jump over them to get across the room.

FITNESS FACTOR: Strength, Cardio, Balance, Flexibility, Mood Booster!

COVERT CALORIES: He'll burn 36 calories in 10 minutes.

SNEAKY SUPERCHARGE: Have him navigate from piece of furniture to piece of furniture without touching the ground. For littler kids, put couch cushions on the ground for them to jump on instead.

#48: Smart Cookies

Mixing and rolling out dough with a rolling pin can burn calories, meaning that you can let your little pastry chef taste what she's made guilt-free.

What you'll need: Cookie dough, rolling pin

Who's playing: Preschoolers, Grade-Schoolers, Tweens

How many: 1 or more

Prime time: Any Day, Rainy Days, Playdates, Weekends

Pick out a cookie recipe and put your child in charge of whisking, mixing, and rolling the cookie dough, cutting the cookies, and putting them on the baking sheet.

FITNESS FACTOR: Cardio, Strength, Mood Booster!

COVERT CALORIES: She'll burn 109 calories in 60 minutes.

SNEAKY SUPERCHARGE: Double the recipe! Make cookies for a party or make an extra batch to store in the freezer.

SAFETY PRECAUTIONS: Monitor your baker closely and be sure that you're the one using the oven.

#49: Pick Your Own

When Larysa was a kid, all of her friends would go strawberry or blueberry picking, but her mom would take her to pick asparagus. Yuck! As an adult she appreciates the veggie's taste but also the fact that it was a harder crop to pick, as it involved bending to get to the root.

What you'll need: A pick-your-own farm (check out www.pickyourown.org for ones near you)

Who's playing: Preschoolers, Grade-Schoolers, Tweens

How many: 1 or more

Prime time: Sunny Days, Weekends, Playdates

Take a road trip to a pick-your-own fruit farm. Apples, pumpkins, pears, peaches and berries will give kids of every age a chance to help. Not only will your kids keep moving as they pluck the fruit, but they'll also be more likely to eat the fruit if they've harvested it themselves.

FITNESS FACTOR: Cardio, Strength, Balance, Flexibility, Mood Booster!

COVERT CALORIES: They'll burn 82 calories in 60 minutes.

SNEAKY SUPERCHARGE: Go high and low—pick veggies and berries that are low to the ground so they have to bend, and then pick fruit on trees so they have to reach.

Excuse Buster!

Your young couch potatoes are sacked out in front of the TV. "Go outside and play," you say. "But I want to watch this show!" they protest. Keep the TV tug-of-war from ruining your day. Instead, nip their excuses in the bud with these easy tricks:

1. Invite a friend over. Grade-schoolers are less likely to lie around if they've got a pal to play with.

2. Unplug the electronics before they get home. If they can't click it on with a press of a button, you'll have a chance to divert their attention before they settle in.

3. Ask for a favor. Grade-schoolers still want to please their parents. Take advantage of their helpful spirits by posing the activity as if the child were doing you a favor. For example, "Austin, I'm trying to think of some cool ways to get in shape. You're looking strong. Can you show me what you've been doing in gym class with Mr. K.? I'd love your help."

#50: Tickle Torture

Nothing makes a mom's heart swell quite like the sound of her children's laughter. Knowing that their giggles mean they're running and keeping their hearts healthy makes it even sweeter.

What you'll need: A willing parent

Who's playing: Preschoolers, Grade-Schoolers

How many: 1 or more

Prime time: Rainy Days

Play "tickle torture," by chasing your kids around the house. When you catch them, start tickling!

FITNESS FACTOR: Cardio, Strength, Mood Booster!

COVERT CALORIES: They'll burn 42 calories in 20 minutes.

Sneaky Supercharge: Turn the game around and have your kids chase you!

Fun fact! Laughing is good for the body and the soul. A giggle fit can burn 20 percent more calories than a straight face would.

#51: Musical Chairs

It's always a challenge to get your kids moving when the television's on. We try to play games during the commercials. Kids get to watch their favorite show and the parents know they're moving. It's a win-win!

What you'll need: Just the furniture in your television room.

Who's playing: Preschoolers, Grade-Schoolers, Tweens

How many: 1 or more

Prime time: Any Day, Rainy Days

Every time a commercial break comes on the television, have everyone stand up and throw a pillow on someone's chair. That chair is "out of play." March around the room until the show comes back on. The person left standing has to stand until the next commercial break.

FITNESS FACTOR: Cardio

COVERT CALORIES: They'll burn 28 calories per 20 minutes.

SNEAKY SUPERCHARGE: Have the person who is left standing "sit" against the wall (his or her back to the wall and knees at a right angle) until the next commercial comes on, which adds a dose of strength training.

#52: Couch Potato

Television has become a competitive sport at our houses!

What you'll need: A pillow or ball

Who's playing: Preschoolers, Grade-Schoolers, Tweens

How many: 2 or more

Prime time: Every Day

When a commercial comes on, play hot potato! Pass the "potato" (the pillow or ball) from one person to another until the show comes back on. Whoever is left holding the potato has to stand until the next commercial comes back on.

• • • • •

FITNESS FACTOR: Cardio, Coordination

COVERT CALORIES: Everyone will burn 23 calories in 20 minutes.

SNEAKY SUPERCHARGE: The person left with the pillow has to stand while balancing it on her head, which will help develop balance and core strength.

Quick Tip!

Does it seem like every time your kids sit down to watch television, they've got their hand in a bag of chips? Our sneaky solution: Keep their hands busy, so they won't be tempted to mindlessly graze. Have them keep active in front of the tube by encouraging them to draw, color, play with play dough, bead, text, build Legos or models, trade Pokemon cards, or weave friendship bracelets to name a few!

#53: No-Skate Hockey

You won't need a rink or skates to play this fast-paced hockey game!

What you'll need: A table, wooden spoons, ice cubes, plastic cups

Who's playing: Grade-Schoolers

How many: 2

Prime time: Sunny Days, Playdates

Use a picnic table as the "ice", and ice cubes as pucks. Hand each player a wooden spoon to use as a stick. If a player shoots the ice cube past the other player off the short side of the table, he scores a point.

• • • • •

FITNESS FACTOR: Cardio, Coordination

COVERT CALORIES: They'll burn 54 calories in 30 minutes.

SNEAKY SUPERCHARGE: Challenge the players to catch the cubes with a plastic cup as they are shot off the table.

Active Party Ideas

Looking for a venue for your child's next birthday? Opt for a party that will keep kids moving. Plus, they'll have burned off so much energy they'll arrive home happy, healthy, and tired out! Here are some of our favorites:

- Martial arts gym
- Ice-skating rink
- Yoga studio
- Batting cages/driving range
- Kiddie gym
- Ballet studio
- Laser tag venue

#54: The Amazing Race

Sometimes it seems as if it's the moms who get the workout at bedtime! Missy says it seems as if the minute the lights go off and her head hits the pillow, someone asks for a glass of water, sending her downstairs and back up. Instead of thinking of it as a stall tactic, she considers it extra exercise for her!

What you'll need: Pajamas, toothbrushes, and other good night items

Who's playing: Grade-Schoolers

How many: 1 or more

Prime time: Every Day

Send your kids on an evening scavenger hunt. Hide their PJs, favorite bedtime story book, toothbrush, and any other item essential to your kids' nighttime routine. Challenge them to find and use all the items and climb into bed as quickly as she can.

FITNESS FACTOR: Cardio, Flexibility

COVERT CALORIES: She'll burn 34 calories in 15 minutes.

SNEAKY SUPERCHARGE: Boost her coordination by having her do a "victory" dance of her own design when she finds all the items.

#55: Go Carts

Just because you don't see exercise on your grocery list doesn't mean it can't be found at the market. Resist the temptation to get in and out of the store as fast as possible and look at it as an opportunity to let your kid burn some energy.

What you'll need: A shopping cart

Who's playing: Grade-Schoolers

How many: 1 or more

Prime time: Any Day

Challenge your child to push the grocery cart, keeping a careful eye that he doesn't bump into anything—or anyone.

FITNESS FACTOR: Strength, Cardio

COVERT CALORIES: He'll burn more than a calorie a minute!

SNEAKY SUPERCHARGE: Hand him canned goods to put into the cart, or ask him to carry a few cans as you walk up and down the aisles together.

#56: Showtime!

Dress up and perform? School-aged kids will be the first to sign up! For the most part, they aren't shy, love the spotlight, and really get into creating routines and stories.

What you'll need: Music, costumes (optional)

Who's playing: Grade-Schoolers

How many: 1 or more

Prime time: Any Day, Rainy Days, Playdates

Have your budding star put on a dance show. Help your child figure out what type of music will get her toes tapping. Let her practice a routine that involves pliés, twirls, jumps, and spins. When she's ready, gather a crowd of family and friends and get ready for a grand performance!

FITNESS FACTOR: Cardio, Flexibility, Balance, Coordination, Mood Booster!

COVERT CALORIES: Your stars will be burning a little more than 20 calories every 10 minutes.

SNEAKY SUPERCHARGE: Keep her attention and keep her dancing longer by having her pick three different types of dancing. Some of our favorites: tap, ballet, belly dancing, hula dancing, folk dancing, Irish dancing, and swing dancing.

#57: Slap Shot!

To give them incentive to play faster, have your children do this activity on an extra hot day, so the "puck" melts quickly.

What you'll need: A large ice cube, brooms

Who's playing: Grade-Schoolers, Tweens

How many: 2 or more

Prime time: Sunny Days, Playdates, Weekends

Freeze water in a 1-quart plastic bowl. Then send your kids to the driveway with two brooms. Using the ice cube as a puck, challenge them to hit the ice past each other to score a goal. Play until the puck melts!

• • • • •

FITNESS FACTOR: Cardio, Strength, Coordination, Mood Booster!

COVERT CALORIES: This burns a whopping 218 calories per hour of play.

SNEAKY SUPERCHARGE: One of Larysa's clients ramps up the intensity by letting her kids play this game on rollerblades, which also helps to improve balance.

Sports with Oomph!

If your kids express an interest in playing a sport, why not steer them to ones that burn the most calories per minute? The following sports will burn more than 100 calories per half hour.

- Tennis
- Swimming
- Soccer
- Track
- Racquetball
- Martial arts
- Hockey
- Football
- Basketball

#58: So You Wanna Be a Rock Star?

It's official: We have entered the world of YouTube. Even if your kids don't post their videos for the world to see, they love to put themselves on camera. Missy's girls are real hams. Recently, they took turns behind and in front of the camera for over an hour.

What you'll need: Music, a video camera, costumes (optional)

Who's playing: Grade-Schoolers, Tweens

How many: 1 or more

Prime time: Any Day, Playdates, Parties, Weekends

Have your child make her own rock video by herself or with her friends. She can pick out her favorite video for inspiration and imitate the moves, setting, and clothing, or she can create a video that's all her own, choreographing her own dancing and coming up with a theme for the stage and outfits. When it's done, gather the gang around for a "premiere."

FITNESS FACTOR: Cardio, Flexibility, Balance, Coordination, Mood Booster!

COVERT CALORIES: Your rocker will burn 123 calories for every hour of filming.

SNEAKY SUPERCHARGE: Have her make a video "montage" by filming a few videos of her doing favorite dances and mixing the clips into a Greatest Hits show.

Wii® Workout

Like many parents, we've given in to the Wii® phenomenon. And while the Wii® Sports games are more active than regular video games that keep your kids glued to the couch, they aren't as active as we'd like them to be. Use the power of the Wii® to convince your kids they'll improve their scores by doing a few exercises prior to playing. Do them together as a family to increase the competition.

TENNIS

Arm circles will build up stamina in the upper body to smash serves. Place your arms straight out from your body, forming a "T," and make small circles backward 20 times and forward 20 times.

GOLF

Flexibility in your core will give you range of motion to let the ball fly down the fairway. Do toe touches by placing your arms out to side, forming a "T." Raise a leg to hip height and touch your opposite arm to your raised toe. Repeat 20 times, alternating legs.

BASEBALL

Do two sets of squats, which will give you the power to hit home runs. Place your feet hip distant apart with toes facing forward. Stick your tush behind you and bend your knees until they are at a right angle. Pitch chest over slightly. Repeat for 10 repetitions and 2 sets.

BOXING

Boxers jump rope to keep their stamina up for long rounds. Pretend that you're holding a jump rope and proceed to "jump rope" for 1 minute for a total of 2 intervals.

BOWLING

Bowlers have to lunge forward with power and flexibility to get strikes. Bend your back knee to ground, keeping your front knee over your ankle—don't move your knee past your toe. Repeat 10 times with both legs.

#59: Just Bag It

Larysa's son Nicholas loves to be in charge of bagging the groceries, especially at the self-checkout machine, since it makes him feel very grown up.

What you'll need: The items on your grocery list

Who's playing: Grade-Schoolers, Tweens

How many: 1 or more

Prime time: Any Day

Put your child in charge of the grocery bags, from bagging and weighing the produce to putting the groceries on the checkout belt to loading the groceries in and out of the car.

FITNESS FACTOR: Strength, Cardio

COVERT CALORIES: He'll burn 23 calories every 20 minutes.

SNEAKY SUPERCHARGE: Hand him different items, like one pound of apples and an 8-oz. can, and ask him to tell you which is heavier.

SAFETY PRECAUTIONS: Keep a close eye on your helper when in the parking lot while he's loading the groceries into the car.

Fun fact! According the EPA, 500 billion to one trillion plastic bags are used every year and pollute our earth. Use reusable bags instead!

#60: Hip Hop

Let your child jump her way to fitness—without skipping a step.

What you'll need: Chalk or masking tape

Who's playing: Grade-Schoolers, Tweens

How many: 1 or more

Prime time: Every Day, Rainy Days

Use chalk or masking tape to outline a hopscotch game on a well-trafficked area like your kitchen, hallway, or basement floor. Tell her she has to hopscotch every time she passes through. Be sure to remove the tape at the end of the day so it doesn't leave a mark.

FITNESS FACTOR: Cardio, Balance, Coordination, Mood Booster!

COVERT CALORIES: She'll burn 27 calories in 15 minutes.

SNEAKY SUPERCHARGE: Expand the hopscotch grid so that it is 20 squares long. Or, add others elsewhere in the house.

#61: Backyard Bowling

This activity is good for your child and the earth. Gather plastic soda or water bottles to recycle, but before you bring them to the curb, use them!

What you'll need: Plastic soda or water bottles (empty), a ball

Who's playing: Grade-Schoolers, Tweens

How many: 1 or more

Prime time: Sunny Days, Playdates, Weekends

Set the water bottles on a flat surface as pins. Give each child two chances to knock down the pins with a ball before switching to the next player.

FITNESS FACTOR: Cardio, Flexibility, Balance, Coordination

COVERT CALORIES: They'll burn 20 calories in 30 minutes.

SNEAKY SUPERCHARGE: Fill the bottles with a little water so they're harder to knock over, requiring even more strength.

Fun fact! Historians believe that bowling is one of the oldest sports, dating back to the cavemen, who may have played a rudimentary version with rocks and pebbles.

#62: Walk Like an Italian

The Italians certainly know their way around a healthy kitchen. It turns out they're also experts when it comes to sneaking in fitness. Parents in Lecco, Italy, have given up on school buses in favor of a piedibus, which translates to" foot bus." It keeps their kids in shape and helps the environment.

What you'll need: Your kids, willing neighbors (optional)

Who's playing: Grade-Schoolers, Tweens

How many: 1 or more

Prime time: Every Day

Skip the school bus and walk your child to school. Recruit neighbors to come along.

• • • • •

FITNESS FACTOR: Cardio

COVERT CALORIES: Your walkers will burn over a calorie per minute.

SNEAKY SUPERCHARGE: Have the kids dribble a basketball as they go, which will also build coordination.

SAFETY PRECAUTIONS: As always, if you're walking where there aren't sidewalks, keep a close eye on your kids.

Q: How do I make fitness cool?

A: Tweens are really into imitating their idols. Figure out the role model (celebrity, pop star, political figure, or athlete) that your child thinks is cool and find out what he or she does to keep fit—in an age of tabloids and blogs it shouldn't take too much research. Then find a way that your kid can do some of the same activities.

#63: Bus Stop Hop

Don't just stand there—make use of the time you have waiting for the school bus. As an added bonus, this will also keep your child warm as she waits in the winter.

What you'll need: Your kids!

Who's playing: Grade-Schoolers

How many: 1 or more

Prime time: Every Day

Act out the lyrics to "The Wheels on the Bus" with littler kids. Older kids can use the curb as a balance beam, pausing to do calf-raises on either end.

FITNESS FACTOR: Cardio, Balance, Coordination, Strength, Mood Booster!

COVERT CALORIES: Burn 28 calories for every 15 minutes of waiting time.

SNEAKY SUPERCHARGE: Littler kids can act out more active songs like "Head, Shoulders, Knees, and Toes" and "Simon Says." Time your older kids to see how many times they can jump in 30 seconds.

SAFETY PRECAUTIONS: As always, if you're near a street, keep a close eye on your kids.

#64: Obstacle Course

Who needs a jungle gym when the contents of your house will do just as well?

What you'll need: The contents of your house

Who's playing: Grade-Schoolers, Tweens

How many: 1 or more

Prime time: Rainy Days, Playdates, Weekends

Help your kids plan an obstacle course. Have them roll under tables, jump from couch cushions, jump on the bed, leap to touch a door jam, roll a ball down a hallway with their nose, walk up the stairs backward, or any other feat they can think of (within reason, of course).

FITNESS FACTOR: Cardio, Flexibility, Balance, Coordination, Strength, Mood Booster!

COVERT CALORIES: They'll burn 45 calories in 10 minutes.

SNEAKY SUPERCHARGE: Have them prep by stretching for 10 minutes before the race begins, which will add 11 calories. Or, have them run the course 5 times, and time each lap to see what their best time is.

#65: Little Red Wagon

Get your child moving, and help the community too.

What you'll need: A wagon or stroller

Who's playing: Grade-Schoolers, Tweens

How many: 1 or more

Prime time: Sunny Days, Weekends

Give your child a hand with collecting items to donate to charity, door-to-door in your neighborhood. Used books, old clothes, and canned food can all be donated to local organizations. Walk from house to house, collecting the donations in a wagon or carriage. Be sure to let him load, pull, and unload the wagon himself.

FITNESS FACTOR: Cardio, Strength, Mood Booster!

COVERT CALORIES: He'll burn 93 calories in 30 minutes.

SNEAKY SUPERCHARGE: Put a younger sibling or pet in the wagon for your child to pull along. Or, make frequent trips home to drop off the stuff.

Quick Tip!

Looking for ideas for how kids and families can donate their time? Try thevolunteerfamily.org and blossominternational.org.

Classic Games with a Sneaky Twist

These games are tried and true, but they could offer your child a chance for even more exercise with a few clever additions.

■ **SIMON SAYS:** Speed up how often you instruct them to touch their toes, nose, ears, etc. Give the game an extra boost by throwing jumping, hopping, and running into the mix.

■ **RED LIGHT, GREEN LIGHT:** Make it a little harder by having the stoplight stand farther from the player each round.

■ **CAPTURE THE DRAGON'S EGG:** This game works best with four or more kids, but two kids can play it as well. Place an "egg" (it can be a real egg or a ball) on a cone or chair. Each team or player must guard their egg from being stolen by the other team. Each child has a "flag" (a scarf or rag or even a sock) tucked into his waistband. The defensive team can get the child on the offensive team "out" by pulling out the defensive team's flag. (If you have enough players, send the ones who are "out" to a dungeon where their teammates can rescue them by tagging them.) The first team to capture a Dragon's Egg wins.

■ **DODGE BALL:** Two classes can play this game. Set up a space to be the defenders' "pen." The offensive players must try to hit the defenders with soft balls within one minute without stepping into the defenders' pen. If a defender catches the ball, the players switch positions. Give the game a boost by using the same number of balls as there are players. Line up the balls in the center of the field and line the players up on the opposite ends. Blow a whistle and have the kids sprint to the center line to grab a ball to throw at the opposite team. Balls get thrown back and forth until a person gets hit with a ball or a ball they have thrown gets caught—those players are declared "out." The last person standing's team wins. (Instruct the players to aim below the shoulder, so no one gets hit in the head.)

Q: How can I help my kids to burn off cooped-up energy after they've been sitting at a desk all day?

A: Channel your inner Girl Scout and be prepared! Have some activities up your sleeve (like arts and crafts, gardening, helping you make dinner) for them to start as soon as they arrive home. You can give them a quick snack if they're hungry but be sure to catch their interest before they plop in front of the television or computer, because once they're there, it's hard to pry them away. Once they've exercised and fueled their bodies they'll be better able to concentrate on their homework. And you can give yourself a Healthy Mom Badge!

#66: Baby You Can Drive This Car

Who cares what the gas prices are these days—this ride burns calories, not petroleum.

What you'll need: Sand, a shovel, and a sand bucket

Who's playing: Grade-Schoolers, Tweens

How many: 1 or more

Prime time: Sunny Days, Weekends

Forget sand castles at the beach—have your kids make a big mound of sand and shape it into a convertible big enough for them to sit in and "drive."

FITNESS FACTOR: Strength, Cardio, Flexibility

COVERT CALORIES: They'll burn 100 calories every hour they build.

SNEAKY SUPERCHARGE: Fill 'er up. Have your kids go back and forth from the water, bringing back buckets of seawater to use as "gas."

SAFETY PRECAUTIONS: As always, keep a close eye on your children when they are playing near water.

#67: Chore Time!

You may have been giving your child an allowance since she was small, but if you haven't, the timing may be right to start now. Not only will it help her develop a sense of fiscal responsibility (and who couldn't use that these days?), but it will also be a great motivator for her to move, as children are apt to do chores without complaining when they are given a small allowance or an incentive (like a slumber party, a day off from doing the dishes, etc). This activity is also a Mommy Mood Booster!

What you'll need: Dust rags, cleaning products, a vacuum cleaner, broom, etc.

Who's playing: Grade-Schoolers, Tweens

How many: 1 or more

Prime time: Any Day, Weekends

Let your kids earn their keep while burning calories: Give them chores that require them to move, stretch, and lift like dusting, vacuuming, sweeping, making the bed, loading and unloading the dishwasher, and taking out the trash.

FITNESS FACTOR: Cardio, Strength

COVERT CALORIES:

· Dusting burns 68 calories in 60 minutes

· Vacuuming will burn 95 calories in 60 minutes

· Sweeping burns 90 calories in 60 minutes

· Loading and unloading the dishwasher racks up 48 calories in 30 minutes

· Taking out the trash will burn almost a calorie per minute

SNEAKY SUPERCHARGE: Work to music, challenging them to finish their task before the song ends.

SAFETY PRECAUTIONS: If you're concerned about caustic cleaning products, opt for natural cleaners with ingredients like vinegar and baking soda.

#68: Green Thumbs

Gardening is not only a strenuous activity, it also teaches children responsibility, patience, biology, and ecology. And as an added bonus, we've realized that kids are more likely to eat veggies if they've grown the greenery themselves, sometimes even right off the vine!

What you'll need: A plot, plants, watering can, gardening trowel

Who's playing: Grade-Schoolers, Tweens

How many: 1 or more

Prime time: Sunny Days, Weekends

Help your child plant a garden. Let him pick out the seeds and plants, determine the layout, and plant and tend to the garden. It's a never-ending workout that can last all year round in many parts of the country. Use the Internet to research what grows best in your climate and what kind of care certain plants need. Best of all, your child will see results from all his hard work—in the garden and in the way he feels.

FITNESS FACTOR: Strength, Cardio, Flexibility, Mood Booster!

COVERT CALORIES: In an hour, your garden guru will burn more than 125 calories per hour, whether he's digging, planting, weeding, or watering.

SNEAKY SUPERCHARGE: Have him use a wheelbarrow to transport plants, fruit, veggies, or weeds.

#69: Go Green

Nicholas loves to recycle, but not the way you think. He takes his metal detector to the beach and then uses his "treasures" to make robots.

What you'll need: Newspapers, cans, bottles, plastic containers, twine, scissors

Who's playing: Grade-Schoolers, Tweens

How many: 1 or more

Prime time: Any Day

Put your child in charge of recycling: Have him stack and tie up the newspapers and magazines; sort the empty bottles and cans into glass, plastic, and metal; and bring the containers to the curb or help you load them in the car and unload them at the recycling center.

FITNESS FACTOR: Cardio, Strength, Flexibility

COVERT CALORIES: He'll burn 54 calories every half hour.

SNEAKY SUPERCHARGE: Tell him he'll get 5 cents for each bottle he recycles (either by bringing it to a store with bottle and can deposits or from you). Watch his environmental enthusiasm skyrocket!

#70: Your American Idol

Just because your child may not have all of America calling in to vote for her, doesn't mean she has to shelve her rock star dreams. Plus, she'll be so busy jumping and dancing and singing that she won't notice how much her heart will be pumping.

What you'll need: Musical instruments

Who's playing: Grade-Schoolers, Tweens

How many: 1 or more

Prime time: Any Day, Rainy Days,
    Playdates, Weekends, Parties

Have her and her buddies form a band, which may not be great for your eardrums, but is a terrific way to get them energized while burning tons of calories. Let them make up their own songs or play their favorites to sing along to.

FITNESS FACTOR: Cardio, Coordination, Mood Booster!

COVERT CALORIES: In a half hour your child could burn:

- 27 calories playing the cello
- 24 on the accordion
- 27 playing the guitar sitting
- 41 playing it standing
- 34 on the violin and the piano
- 27 playing the flute
- 54 playing the drums
- 48 on the trombone
- 34 on the trumpet

SNEAKY SUPERCHARGE: Ask the band to play rock music, swing, or '50s tunes, all of which burn more calories than other dance styles.

#71: Top Chef

Throwing a dinner party can be a lot of work! Mixing, rolling, and beating can burn lots of calories, which any mom or dad who entertains even the smallest of guests already knows.

What you'll need: A recipe, ingredients, kitchen equipment

Who's playing: Grade-Schoolers, Tweens

How many: 1 or more

Prime time: Any Day, Playdates, Weekends

Give yourself a break from making a meal and put your kids in charge. Help them select the menu for the family (see Missy's Sneaky Chef recipes for inspiration—keeping the secret ingredient under wraps, of course).

FITNESS FACTOR: Strength, Cardio, Mood Booster!

COVERT CALORIES: They'll burn a calorie for every minute on their feet.

SNEAKY SUPERCHARGE: Remind them that making the meal also means setting the table and cleaning up, which burns an additional 23 calories.

SAFETY PRECAUTIONS: Oversee their culinary endeavors when you need to, particularly if they're using knives or the stovetop.

Foods That Require a Little Muscle

It's possible to burn some calories BEFORE you eat. The following foods require a little effort while you prepare them. Mix them into your little sous chef's menus whenever you can.

- Get the ingredients out of the fridge and pantry
- Peel the potatoes and carrots
- Spin the salad in a salad spinner
- Shake up some dressing for a salad

- Use a rolling pin to flatten cookie dough
- Knead some bread
- Mash potatoes with a masher or ricer
- Pound meat with a mallet
- Stir risotto in a pot
- Beat egg whites by hand with a whisk for meringue
- Beat cream with a whisk to make whipped cream

#72: Make a Splash!

Pools and lakes can provide the whole family with endless hours of fun. Larysa plays this game with her family every summer. Someone pretends to be the announcer, and the kids pretend they're at the Olympics. They choose their names and what country they are representing. For example, "Next up, Lucy Lovebug from Sweden. She'll be doing her signature wacky twist jump."

What you'll need: A pool and some eager swimmers

Who's playing: Grade-Schoolers, Tweens

How many: 1 or more

Prime time: Sunny Days, Weekends, Playdates

Hold a dive or jump contest: Kids will get creative as they leap into the deep end. Kids and adults can rate each jump from 1 to 10.

FITNESS FACTOR: Cardio, Balance, Flexibility, Coordination, Strength, Mood Booster!

COVERT CALORIES: Your Olympic hopefuls will burn 82 calories in 60 minutes.

SNEAKY SUPERCHARGE: Have each competitor swim a victory lap after each jump.

• Breast stroke will burn an extra 136 calories

• Freestyle will burn 109

• Backstroke 95

• Butterfly 150

SAFETY PRECAUTIONS: As always when your children are playing near water, keep a careful eye on them. Do not let them dive into shallow water.

#73: Search & Dive

This activity is fun for adults and kids alike!

What you'll need: Coins and/or a watermelon, a pool

Who's playing: Grade-Schoolers, Tweens

How many: 1 or more

Prime time: Sunny Days, Playdates, Parties, Weekends

Toss coins in the pool for kids to retrieve. Want some laughs? Grease a watermelon with vegetable shortening and throw it in the pool. Challenge kids and adults to capture it and bring it to the pool deck.

FITNESS FACTOR: Cardio, Coordination, Mood Booster!

COVERT CALORIES: This will burn 177 calories in 60 minutes.

SNEAKY SUPERCHARGE: Grease a few mini-watermelons and see who can get to the other end of the pool carrying one first, which will give an added boost of strength and balance.

SAFETY PRECAUTIONS: As always when your children are playing near or in water, keep a careful eye on them. Do not allow them to dive into shallow water, and never toss coins near the pool drain.

Sneaky Swaps!

These activities are ones kids already love. Why not supercharge them? All calories calculated for one hour of activity. Here's how:

SPORT:	SUPERCHARGE:
Doubles tennis (163 calories)	Singles tennis (218 calories)
Water volleyball (82 calories)	Beach volleyball (218 calories)
Backstroke (191 calories)	Butterfly (300 calories)
Downhill skiing (164 calories)	Cross-country skiing (191 calories)
Running on a flat surface (245 calories)	Running up stairs (409 calories)
Golfing with a cart (95 calories)	Golfing carrying clubs (123 calories)
Leisure biking (109 calories)	Mountain biking (232 calories)

#74: Surreptitious Charades

This is also a great way to slip in some exercise when you're away from home, in a hotel or waiting for your flight at the airport.

What you'll need: Index cards or slips of paper, pen or pencil

Who's playing: Grade-Schoolers, Tweens

How many: 1 or more

Prime time: Any Day, Rainy Days, Playdates, Parties

Play charades—with a sneaky twist. Write down subjects that involve a lot of action, like animals, sports, or activities for kids to act out.

FITNESS FACTOR: Cardio, Coordination, Flexibility

COVERT CALORIES: Your players will burn 109 calories in an hour.

SNEAKY SUPERCHARGE: Have them use couch cushions as a stage. The uneven surface will help improve their strength and balance.

#75: Little Squirts

We're not big fans of "gun play" at our houses, but when the temperature rises, we're willing to make an exception—as long as they're aiming at the target, and not at each other.

What you'll need: Water pistols, chalk

Who's playing: Grade-Schoolers, Tweens

How many: 1 or more

Prime time: Sunny Days, Playdates

Draw a circular target on a wall or tree trunk. Challenge your little sharpshooters to hit the bull's eye with water guns. For a more aerobic game, you can set up a series of targets across your lawn and have them run to each one.

FITNESS FACTOR: Coordination

COVERT CALORIES: He'll burn 34 calories in a half hour.

SNEAKY SUPERCHARGE: Use a super-soaker, which will make him pump his arms, or give it a cardio and strength boost by throwing water balloons at a target instead.

#76: Sneaky Southpaw

This activity may not burn many calories but it will give your kids a big coordination boost. It's also harder than it looks. Try it yourself and show your kids how it challenges even you.

What you'll need: Toothbrush, toothpaste

Who's playing: Grade-Schoolers, Tweens

How many: 1 or more

Prime time: Any day

Help her build her coordination by challenging her to brush her teeth with her non-dominant hand (her right if she's a lefty, her left if she's a righty).

FITNESS FACTOR: Coordination

COVERT CALORIES: She'll burn 9 calories in 10 minutes.

SNEAKY SUPERCHARGE: Ask her to stand on one foot while she brushes, which will add coordination, strength, and balance.

#77: Basket Cases

Never miss a chance to encourage your kid to do a little heavy lifting. When Sammy was a pre-schooler, Missy would bring her to the store and Sammy would use her little eco-friendly tote bag as a basket.

What you'll need: A grocery basket (or two)

Who's playing: Grade-Schoolers, Tweens

How many: 1 or more

Prime time: Any day

Skip the grocery cart and hand your child a basket to carry instead. Better yet, hand her two—one for each hand!

FITNESS FACTOR: Strength, Cardio

COVERT CALORIES: She'll burn 68 calories in an hour.

SNEAKY SUPERCHARGE: When her basket is full or too heavy, transfer the items to Mom's cart so she can refill the basket.

#78: On a Roll

Larysa recommends that you plant items like rubber balls, balance balls, Bosus, and hippety hops in your TV room, so kids will naturally play on them while watching their favorite shows.

What you'll need: A soft ball, between the size of a basketball and a softball

Who's playing: Grade-Schoolers, Tweens

How many: 1 or more

Prime time: Any Day, Rainy Days

When your child is sitting and watching TV, challenge him to place a ball on his ankles, with legs together, and see if he can lift his legs and roll the ball up to his thighs.

FITNESS FACTOR: Strength

COVERT CALORIES: He'll burn 34 calories in 20 minutes.

SNEAKY SUPERCHARGE: Increase the cardio and coordination factor by putting the ball aside and placing two whoopee cushions side by side on the couch. Have him jump back and forth between them—giggles will follow.

Quick Tip!

Long day? Ask your child for a back massage, she'll burn 27 calories in 15 minutes!

#79: Slip and Slide

Missy's latest sneaky purchase was bright green "dust mop slippers." They didn't stay bright green for long, though, as she and her girls saw who could make them the dirtiest by sliding all over the kitchen and foyer. Every time they slip and slide, they get a great workout, and the house ends up gleaming.

What you'll need: A pair of old socks

Who's playing: Grade-Schoolers, Tweens

How many: 1 or more

Prime time: Any Day, Rainy Days

Put on some old socks and let your kids slip and slide while they dust the floors.

FITNESS FACTOR: Cardio, Balance, Strength, Mood Booster!

COVERT CALORIES: They'll burn 68 calories in 30 minutes.

SNEAKY SUPERCHARGE: Add a little coordination and amp up the pace by putting on "The Twist" and have them twist and slide as they go, which will also tack on an extra 33 calories for every 15 minutes they dance.

#80: Main Squeeze

Test your child's strength—without having to turn off the TV. (You can also use it as an anger management tool—Missy asked her daughter, Samantha, to show her how angry she was one day, by asking her to try to "break" a tennis ball.)

What you'll need: A soccer ball

Who's playing: Grade-Schoolers, Tweens

How many: 1

Prime time: Any day

Challenge her to see if she can "break" a soccer ball by squeezing it tightly between her knees while sitting down.

FITNESS FACTOR: Strength

COVERT CALORIES: She'll burn 32 calories in 20 minutes.

SNEAKY SUPERCHARGE: Challenge her to hold the ball between her legs, release it, then catch it again between her legs without dropping it, which will help her develop coordination.

#81: Community Clean-Up

Many towns hold a spring clean-up volunteer day, but you can do your part to spruce up the neighborhood any time.

What you'll need: Garbage bags, gloves

Who's playing: Grade-Schoolers, Tweens

How many: 1 or more

Prime time: Sunny Days, Weekends

Have your child don gloves and play "Agent Green" and help him pick up litter in public areas. Give your kids a point for each piece they dispose of and see who gets the most number of points.

FITNESS FACTOR: Cardio, Flexibility

COVERT CALORIES: He'll burn 82 calories in 60 minutes.

SNEAKY SUPERCHARGE: Give him even more incentive—promise to pay him a nickel for each point.

SAFETY PRECAUTIONS: Keep a careful eye on your child and be sure she doesn't pick up anything dangerous.

#82: Sneaky Shoelaces

Kids don't take the time to stretch, which means they often have tight hamstrings. This activity is the perfect way to slip in some stretching everyday, helping them become more flexible.

What you'll need: A pair of shoes with laces

Who's playing: Grade-Schoolers, Tweens

How many: 1

Prime time: Every Day

Ask your kids to try to tie their shoes without sitting down or kneeling each time the need to tie them throughout the day.

FITNESS FACTOR: Flexibility

COVERT CALORIES: They'll burn 16 calories in 10 minutes.

SNEAKY SUPERCHARGE: Have them sit on the floor with legs extended and try to tie shoes that way.

#83: Pillow Fight!

Why wait for a slumber party to host a pillow fight? It will generate lots of giggles and burn calories!

What you'll need: Soft pillows

Who's playing: Grade-Schoolers, Tweens

How many: 2 or more

Prime time: Any Day, Parties, Playdates

Host a pillow fight!

FITNESS FACTOR: Cardio, Strength, Balance, Mood Booster!

COVERT CALORIES: Your "fighters" will burn 82 calories in 20 minutes.

SNEAKY SUPERCHARGE: Pile pillows on the floor and have them jump into them.

SAFETY PRECAUTIONS: Be sure you're using soft, pillows and not hard, foam ones.

#84: I'm With the Band

Emily's fifth grade teacher, Mr. Levine, is a drummer, and he'd hold drum circles in their classroom every Friday afternoon. Now Emily runs around the house, drumsticks in hand, tapping all different surfaces as she experiments for her "rock band."

What you'll need: A pair of drumsticks

Who's playing: Grade-Schoolers, Tweens

How many: 1

Prime time: Any Day, Rainy Days

Show your little rocker how to drum on different surfaces—tables, chairs, boxes, pots, and pans.

FITNESS FACTOR: Cardio, Strength, Coordination, Mood Booster!

COVERT CALORIES: She'll burn 109 calories in 60 minutes.

SNEAKY SUPERCHARGE: Have her stand as she drums. Or, put on music and have her pretend to be the drummer as she dances along to the beat.

#85: Anything You Can Do, I Can Do Better

Kids love to see grown-ups act silly—especially if you're struggling to do something that they can do with ease.

What you'll need: Your imagination

Who's playing: Grade-Schoolers, Tweens

How many: 1 or more

Prime time: Any Day, Weekends

Have your child challenge you to do something active like touching toes, making up silly dances, leaping over toys in the backyard, sports moves, or whatever catches his fancy. After you've taken a turn, ask him to show you how it's done.

FITNESS FACTOR: Cardio, Strength, Balance, Flexibility, Coordination

COVERT CALORIES: He'll burn 36 calories in 20 minutes.

SNEAKY SUPERCHARGE: Make an obstacle course that everyone in the family has to do and see who completes it fastest.

#86: Throw for Distance

This is another idea that makes good use of the contents of the recycling bin—and maybe even inspires your kids to be more diligent recyclers.

What you'll need: A ball, empty plastic bottles and cans

Who's playing: Grade-Schoolers, Tweens

How many: 1 or more

Prime time: Sunny Days, Playdates

Challenge your child to see how far she can throw a ball. Then see how accurately she can throw it by setting up bottles and cans a few feet away on the ground, stair, or wall for her to knock down.

FITNESS FACTOR: Coordination, Flexibility

COVERT CALORIES: She'll burn 41 calories in a half hour.

SNEAKY SUPERCHARGE: Move the cans or stand back farther and farther with each round, which will help develop strength.

#87: Bounce, Bounce, Bounce

The only way Larysa could get one of her tween clients to do cardio was to put her on the trampoline. They'd make up routines and challenge each other to do them—it was challenging and fun!

What you'll need: A mini trampoline or balance ball, hippety hop, or balance ball

Who's playing: Grade-Schoolers, Tweens

How many: 1

Prime time: Any Day, Rainy Days

Put the mini trampoline in front of the television and challenge him to see how many jumps he can do during each commercial.

• • • • •

FITNESS FACTOR: Cardio, Balance, Coordination, Mood booster!

COVERT CALORIES: He'll burn 48 calories in a half hour.

SNEAKY SUPERCHARGE: Tell your child that you need his help "breaking in" the trampoline—the more he jumps, the softer it'll become.

Quick Tip!

If your kids ask (okay, beg) to watch just one more show, let them—but tell them they have to jump on the trampoline for the duration of the program. This is one of Missy's favorite tricks for Sammy and Emily! Or strategically place a stationary bike in the TV room.

#88: Memory Moves

*This activity was inspired by the heroine of **Akeelah and the Bee**, as well as research that shows that moving rhythmically and putting words and facts to music helps you remember things. Plus: Exercise boosts blood flow to a brain area involved in memory—all of which will come in handy during homework time!*

What you'll need: A homework assignment

Who's playing: Grade-Schoolers, Tweens

How many: 1

Prime time: Every Day

Help your child memorize her multiplication tables, spelling words, or any other homework assignment by encouraging her to walk around the house as she repeats the words.

FITNESS FACTOR: Cardio

COVERT CALORIES: She'll burn 18 calories in 20 minutes.

SNEAKY SUPERCHARGE: Have her jump rope or do lateral jumps over a tile in your kitchen or floor boards, which will add another 73 calories.

#89: Wake-Up Call

One of Larysa's clients placed her son's alarm clock on the other side of the room to get him moving more quickly in the morning. He complains about it daily, but she's noticed how much more quickly he's dressed and ready.

What you'll need: An alarm clock

Who's playing: Grade-Schoolers, Tweens

How many: 1

Prime time: Every Day

Place your child's alarm clock on the opposite side of his room so he has to walk over to it to turn it off. Not only will it ensure he gets out of bed on time, but he'll also start the day moving!

FITNESS FACTOR: Cardio

COVERT CALORIES: He'll burn 7 calories in 5 minutes.

SNEAKY SUPERCHARGE: Have him wake up to his favorite song and challenge him to make his bed by the time the song ends, which will add another 9 calories to his morning routine.

#90: Remote Control

Remember the days when you actually had to get up to change the channel?

What you'll need: The remote control

Who's playing: Grade-Schoolers, Tweens

How many: 1

Prime time: Every Day

Hide the remote and ask your child to get up to change the channel.

• • • • •

FITNESS FACTOR: Cardio, Strength

COVERT CALORIES: She'll burn 9 calories in 10 minutes.

SNEAKY SUPERCHARGE: Push the couch farther from the television. If she's snacking while watching television, make a rule that she has to put away her dishes right away (and not place them on the table in front of her, so she'll have to get up.)

Fidget Factor

People who fidget can burn up to 800 more calories per day than people who don't, according to the Mayo Clinic in Rochester, Minnesota. So next time your little one keeps getting up and out of her seat, stretches, changes positions or even—dare we say it—pokes a sibling, think of it as exercise, instead of an annoyance!

#91: Homework High-Five

Homework's only a drag if you treat it so. This activity will help spark a little enthusiasm in your favorite student.

What you'll need: A kitchen timer

Who's playing: Grade-Schoolers, Tweens

How many: 1

Prime time: Every Day

While your child is doing homework, set a timer for 10-, 15- or 20-minute intervals. When the timer goes off, have him come to you and give a high-five. It will give him a chance to stretch his legs and give him a sense of accomplishment.

FITNESS FACTOR: Cardio

COVERT CALORIES: He'll burn 14 calories in 5 minutes.

SNEAKY SUPERCHARGE: Make up a "Secret Homework High Five" routine that involves a jump, skip, twist, toe touch, hip check and/or dance, which will help him develop coordination.

#92: Halftime Show

Take it from us—and Missy's kids: Say the words "Hannah Montana" and you won't have to do much prodding to get them to start singing and dancing. Larysa's kids are also big fans of the Power Rangers and like to imitate their moves.

What you'll need: A remote with a mute button

Who's playing: Grade-Schoolers, Tweens

How many: 1 or more

Prime time: Every Day

Every time a commercial comes on, press the mute button and ask your kids to give you a floor show—sing, dance, or act out what just happened in the show they're watching.

FITNESS FACTOR: Cardio, Coordination, Mood Booster!

COVERT CALORIES: They'll burn 41 calories in 20 minutes.

SNEAKY SUPERCHARGE: When the show's over, request a full recap—have them act out all the parts and give you a coming attraction of what they think will happen in the next episode.

#93: Loch Ness Monster

Grandpa Chase and his granddaughters spend hours skipping rocks together on the Long Island Sound—a perfect time for family bonding and a little muscle building.

What you'll need: A lake, bay or calm ocean; flat rocks

Who's playing: Grade-Schoolers, Tweens

How many: 1 or more

Prime time: Sunny Days, Weekends

Teach your children how to skip rocks and see who can throw the farthest, waking up the Loch Ness Monster.

FITNESS FACTOR: Strength, Cardio, Flexibility, Balance, Coordination, Mood Booster!

COVERT CALORIES: They'll burn 34 calories in a half hour.

SNEAKY SUPERCHARGE: Have your children prep by finding and making piles of the flattest rocks, the most round rocks, and the biggest rocks and then have a competition throwing them all, which will burn an extra 37 calories.

SAFETY PRECAUTIONS: Be careful when throwing rocks. Establish a rule that everyone must stand behind the person who is throwing.

#94: Purchasing Power

Fashion- and gadget-conscious tweens can burn extra calories when they've got money burning in their pockets. You've probably been told you can squeeze in some exercise by parking your car a nice distance away from the store—forcing you to walk farther. But you can also slip in some exercise while you and your Tween are shopping, too, with this trick.

What you'll need: A kid with spending money

Who's playing: Tweens

How many: 1 or more

Prime time: Any Day, Rainy Days

After selecting an item you or your child wants to purchase, ask the salesclerk to put the item on hold. Have your child do a lap around the store or the mall. Not only will it be a fitness boost, it will give your child time to consider if he *really* wants this item, and maybe even give him an opportunity to compare prices at a nearby store. That's fit and thrifty!

FITNESS FACTOR: Cardio, Mood Booster!

COVERT CALORIES: Your shoppers will burn 52 calories in 30 minutes.

SNEAKY SUPERCHARGE: Race-walk your child from store to store, which will burn 88 calories every half hour.

Active Party Idea for Tweens

Birthdays are for fun, friends, and fitness! Here's one of our favorite party ideas—your guests will be having such a good time they won't even notice they're getting in a workout.

Arrange a scavenger hunt for items that can be found on your town's main street or in a mall. Missy's daughter Emily attended a party like this recently. Each girl was given a couple of dollars to buy some of the items on the list. They had to gather chopsticks from the local Japanese restaurant, a hanger from the dry cleaner, a magazine from the newsstand, nail polish from the nail salon, and a piece of orange candy, to name a few. The girls were divided into teams, with a mom, dad, or older sibling each supervising a team. The group who arrived at the finish line with all the items on the list won. Because the list wasn't organized by location, they had to run up and down the street a few times. "By the time I picked Emily up a few hours later, she was happily exhausted—and her team won!" reported Missy.

#95: It's a Beautiful Day in the Neighborhood

Helping out a neighbor in need is good for your child's heart in more ways than one. It will teach her the values of kindness, compassion, tolerance, community responsibility, and good citizenship. Surprisingly, it can also keep her in shape!

What you'll need: Neighbor who needs a helping hand

Who's playing: Tweens

How many: 1 or more

Prime time: Any Day, Weekends

Have your child help out an elderly neighbor or a family that's going through a rough patch by raking the lawn, shoveling their walk, taking the newspapers and/or mail to their front door, weeding their garden, and carrying in the groceries.

FITNESS FACTOR: Strength, Cardio, Flexibility, Balance

COVERT CALORIES:

· Raking the lawn burns 59 calories every 30 minutes

· Shoveling the walk will burn 82 in 30 minutes

· Weeding the garden burns more than 2 calories per minute

· Carrying in the groceries burns 34 calories every 30 minutes

· Loading and unloading the car burns 27 per 30 minutes

· Feeding pets burns 23 calories every 20 minutes

SNEAKY SUPERCHARGE: Have your child dedicate one hour a week to helping someone out, which will get her in the habit of lending an active hand.

#96: Adopt a Cause

Larysa has partnered with a local food bank to get parents and kids involved. Called "Will Spin for Food," kids and adults spin (indoor cycle) for a specific amount of time to earn pledges of canned goods and money from other people. The kids have a blast!

What you'll need: A food pantry, community shelter, or soup kitchen

Who's playing: Tweens

How many: 1 or more

Prime time: Any Day, Weekends

Have your kids volunteer at a local food pantry. Sorting and unloading food will have him bending, reaching, and lifting.

FITNESS FACTOR: Cardio, Strength, Flexibility

COVERT CALORIES: Your helpers will burn 109 calories in just a half hour.

SNEAKY SUPERCHARGE: Ask your children to volunteer to set up, serve, and/or clean up meals, which will burn additional calories.

#97: Suds 'R' Us

Getting squirted with water, making huge piles of suds, hanging out with friends—what more would a kid want on a warm day?

What you'll need: A car, a bucket, a hose, sponges, non-phosphate eco-soap

Who's playing: Tweens

How many: 1 or more

Prime time: Sunny Days, Weekends, Playdates

Washing the car will keep them giggling *and* keep them bending, stretching, reaching, and lifting.

• • • • •

FITNESS FACTOR: Cardio, Strength, Flexibility, Balance, Mood Booster!

COVERT CALORIES: In an hour, they'll have burned 82 calories.

SNEAKY SUPERCHARGE: Hold a neighborhood car wash—making the activity last all afternoon, or at least until their fingers look like prunes. Or, tell them not to use the hose, and rely on buckets of water alone.

Tween Playlist

Here are some albums that will have your tweens on the dance floor:

1. Drew's Famous Smash Hits
2. Hannah Montana 2 Non-Stop Dance Party
3. Camp Rock!
4. Aquamarine soundtrack
5. High School Musical 2 soundtrack

#98: Job Joy

By now, your tween is old enough to take on a small, few-hours-a-week job. Not only will it teach responsibility, develop her work ethic, and put some spending money in her pocket, but it will also keep her on her feet.

What you'll need: An employer

Who's playing: Tweens

How many: 1

Prime time: Any Day, Weekends

Help your child find small jobs that will burn big-time calories, such as washing windows, mowing the lawn, mommy's helper, a paper route, snow shoveling, leaf raking, dog walking, and plant watering.

FITNESS FACTOR: Strength, Cardio

COVERT CALORIES: In just a half hour, your worker bee will burn:

- 41 calories washing windows
- 75 calories mowing the lawn
- 55 calories as a mommy's helper
- 82 calories on a paper route and shoveling snow
- 59 calories raking
- 54 calories walking dogs
- 34 watering plants

SNEAKY SUPERCHARGE: Have her figure out long- and short-term goals for the money she makes—the more tangible the goal, the more she'll want to work.

Excuse Buster!

How do I respond to the boredom of my tech-obsessed tween zombie?

There are several sneaky ways to deal with a tween who spends too much time texting or on the computer. Setting limits on how long they can use the computer or TV is the first step. As independent as these kids want to be, they still need—and like—guidelines. Larysa's motto is always, "Out of sight, out of mind." Put away the phone, shut the TV off, and power down the computer. While the technology is in lock-down the rest of the family shouldn't use these devices either. It will be too tempting for a tween to power back up if she sees others doing it.

You can't just tell a tween to "Go out and play." Left on their own, they'll do more "hanging" than playing. So give them a project. We've got plenty for you in this book! Use technology to your advantage. For example, while the computer is still on, have your tween search Google for how to build a go-cart, print out the directions, and go to work.

#99: Walk the Walk, Talk the Talk

When Missy's daughter, Emily, got a cell phone at the beginning of fifth grade, it came with a few rules—one of which was that she's not allowed to put it to her ear. With an earpiece in and her hands free, she's naturally more likely to pace around the house as she chats.

What you'll need: A phone, a headset (optional)

Who's playing: Tweens

How many: 1

Prime time: Every Day

House Rule: If you're chatting on the phone, you have to be up and on your feet. Pacing around the house will help your tween burn some calories.

FITNESS FACTOR: Cardio

COVERT CALORIES: Your chatty child will burn almost a calorie per minute.

SNEAKY SUPERCHARGE: Have her climb the stairs as she talks, which will add 64 calories in a half hour.

#100: Sneaky Fitness
Home Edition

Watch your tween flex her independent spirit while she flexes her muscles. This has become such a regular Sunday activity in Missy's daughter's bedroom that she's gotten really strong from shifting her dresser from one end of the room to the other.

What you'll need: Your child's bedroom

Who's playing: Tweens

How many: 1

Prime time: Rainy Days, Weekends

Help your child rearrange the furniture in her room.

FITNESS FACTOR: Cardio, Strength, Flexibility, Balance

COVERT CALORIES: Moving furniture burns 82 calories in 30 minutes.

SNEAKY SUPERCHARGE: Your tween can also paint stencils on the walls (or paint or wallpaper the back of the door or inside of a closet). Painting and wallpapering add another 82 calories each to the project's tally.

SAFETY PRECAUTIONS: Keep a close eye on your kids if they use ladders or stepstools to paint or wallpaper.

A Day in the Life of a Fit Kid

By now you've seen some of our stealth ideas for weaving exercise effortlessly into your children's everyday life. Soon it will become a habit—slipping in mini-workouts, finding ways to stay active, and hiding healthy ingredients in your kids' favorite foods will become so second nature, you may not even realize you're doing it yourself!

Here's an example of a typical day in the life of a Sneaky Fitness grade-schooler. Let it inspire you!

6:30: He wakes up when his alarm clock starts blaring his favorite tune. Because the clock is placed across the room, he has to get out of bed to shut it off. He makes his bed before the next song ends (#89, Wake-Up Call). His mom comes in and helps him do the Butterfly Flight stretch (page 53) and then challenges him to get dressed against the clock, like a fireman (#24, Fireman Drill).

7:00: While he walks the dog, playing fetch as he goes (#40, Pound Puppy), Mom pops **Get a Move on Muffin Soufflés** (page 187) for him to eat before he goes to school.

7:45: He joins his neighbors as they walk swiftly to school (#62, Walk Like an Italian).

8:15: In school, he takes every other stair between classes (#38, Mountaineers) and plays some supercharged classic playground games at recess (page 85).

12:00: He eats **a Crackle & Pop Peanut Butter Sandwich** (page 211), an apple, and two Sneaker-Doodle Cookies (page 245) at lunch.

3:00: Mom meets him at school and she tells him she wants to "Check out a new route home" that just happens to be a bit longer than their normal route (shh!).

3:30: He walks the dog again.

3:45: He grabs a **Rock 'n' Roll-up Pizza Stick** (page 232) and meets his neighborhood crew to practice their band's latest song (#70, Your American Idol).

5:00: He does his homework—getting a high-five every time he finishes a task (#91, Homework High-Five).

6:15: He sets the table, bringing one plate from the kitchen at a time (#30, Waitress Workout) and then helps you scoop out the potatoes for **Off the Couch Potato Skins** (page 226).

7:00: Your family gathers together to eat dinner, and he helps bring the dishes to the kitchen.

8:00: He watches his favorite show with Mom and Dad, playing #51, Musical Chairs, during the commercial breaks.

8:30: He gets ready for bed by scrambling to find his toothbrush, pajamas and bedtime book as in #54, The Amazing Race.

8:45: He reads a chapter of his book, gets a goodnight kiss from Mom and Dad, and turns out the light!

In one day, this fit kid burned 432 extra calories, which adds up to 3,024 calories a week, 12,960 calories a month, and 157,680 calories a year, which will go a long way toward helping your child maintain his ideal body weight!

His mom and dad rest easy, too, knowing their healthy little boy will sleep well and be ready for another fun, fit day in the morning!

PART TWO

Sneaky Chef Shapes Up

Keeping our kids healthy—and instill-ing good-for-you habits so they'll stay healthy long after they've left the nest—can be daunting. After all, you're battling tele-vision, the computer, video games, and cell phones for their attention; multi-million-dollar marketing campaigns for sugary treats and must-have gadgets for their (okay, your) wallets; and finally, your children themselves, who declare exercise is "boring" and that green veggies are "icky." As Missy's proven with her previous *Sneaky Chef* books and as Larysa's experienced in her gym, the solution is simple—sneak healthy elements into the things your kids *already* like to do and eat every day. Since you'll know she's been burning calories and eating nutrient-rich foods, you won't have to battle her when she objects to flexing her muscles or cleaning her plate. And since you're not making exercise or eating right an issue, you can actually talk with them about the topics in a way that makes them more likely to listen. (The fact that the activities are truly fun and the food is yummy doesn't hurt either!)

This chapter will show you just how to make the most of The Sneaky Chef philosophy in your kitchen and will explain why the 50 new scrumptious recipes that follow will not only get gobbled up by your kids, but will make your life easier to boot.

Just as in Missy's previous books—*The Sneaky Chef: Simple Strategies for Hiding Healthy Foods in Kids Favorite Meals* and *The Sneaky Chef to the Rescue*—the recipes here show you how to hide healthy foods in the meals your kids already love. She uses simple purees of nutrient-dense superfoods like spinach and blueberries (see page 255) and slips them into dishes that are so delish your kids won't know they are there. In addition, she's got clever methods up her sleeve (see page 164) that help distract and delight your kids so they won't focus on the good-for-you factor in the food. She also shares quick tips she's picked up from her own experiences in the kitchen and from the moms around the country she's heard from since her first book landed on the shelves. Missy's a real mom, with real kids, and she continues to offer kid-tested and approved solutions.

The recipes in *Sneaky Fitness* follow in that tradition, but have a few new twists:

They're even easier to make. Missy knows that you're as busy as she is, so she's kept your busy schedule in mind as she's developed these recipes, avoiding meals that take multiple steps, offering suggestions for shortcuts when possible, and keeping the ingredient list to items that you're likely to have on hand, so you won't have to make a separate trip to the market. She's incorporating fewer purees and blends, narrowing them down to her most popular, so you'll have less prep work, too!

They save you time. You can make, freeze, and heat most of these recipes, which means you can whip them up when you've got time to spare and serve them when you don't. Best yet, having breakfast, lunch, dinner, and snacks stocked in your freezer means you'll always have something on hand.

You can grab them and go! Does it seem as if you spend more time in your car than ever before? Eating on the run often means reaching for a pre-packaged, processed snack or fast-food meal that's full of fat, sugar, and sodium—and leaves you craving more later. It's unlikely your lifestyle will suddenly be less mobile, but your family's diet can be a lot healthier while on the road. Many of Missy's new recipes are designed to go from the fridge or microwave straight out the door, so you don't have to give up health for convenience.

They're versatile. We know that kids love anything presented to them in miniature form (see Method #11 below). But did you know that "mini" can appeal to busy moms and dads, too? It does when you're talking about mini-meals: many of these recipes are for smaller menus—meals that can make for a good dinner, a satisfying weekend lunch, or a hearty snack. This allows you to mix and match to suit your family's appetite, no matter how big or how small.

They're built to last. Sugary, simple-carb foods trigger a spike of energy before sharply taking a nosedive, leaving your kids tired, lethargic, and cranky. Missy's recipes—especially the breakfasts featured here—are designed to cause just the opposite effect: the slow burn. The whole grains, veggies, protein, and reduced sugar the recipes call for will result in your kids feeling a more even, longer-lasting energy. They'll be better able to concentrate and their mood will stay on an even keel with this premium-grade fuel.

Our aim is to help you get and keep your children in the race to lifelong good health. These *Sneaky Fitness* recipes will help you make it to the finish line in top form.

SNEAKY STAPLES TO KEEP IN THE KITCHEN

Stock your pantry, fridge, and freezer with the following items and you'll always be ready to cook up any healthy *Sneaky Chef* recipe, no matter what else is on your to-do list. They're all easy to find at your grocery store and you can very often find organic versions as well, if you prefer.

FRESH PRODUCE:
- ☐ **Baby spinach**
- ☐ **Zucchini**
- ☐ **Broccoli**
- ☐ **Sweet potatoes (or yams)**
- ☐ **Cauliflower**
- ☐ **Berries, in season**
- ☐ **Bananas**

- ☐ Avocados
- ☐ Onions
- ☐ Russet potatoes
- ☐ Lemons

MEAT/FISH

- ☐ Beef, lean ground
- ☐ Turkey, lean ground
- ☐ Hot dogs (no nitrates)
- ☐ Fish fillets—tilapia or flounder (ideally not farm-raised)
- ☐ Chicken—skinless, boneless tenders or drumsticks

CEREALS/FLOUR

- ☐ Wheat germ, unsweetened
- ☐ Oat bran
- ☐ Old-fashioned rolled oats (not quick-cooking)
- ☐ Cereal, high-fiber flakes
- ☐ Cereal, brown rice
- ☐ Flour, whole wheat (stone ground)
- ☐ Flour, white (unbleached)
- ☐ Cornmeal
- ☐ Flax seed, ground

RICE/PASTA

- ☐ Brown rice
- ☐ Macaroni and cheese, boxed (ideally without artificial flavors)
- ☐ Whole-grain pasta—elbows and ziti
- ☐ Wonton wrappers
- ☐ Lasagna noodles, "no boil"

BREAD

- ☐ Bread, whole wheat
- ☐ Tortillas, whole wheat
- ☐ Tortillas, corn
- ☐ Bread crumbs, whole wheat
- ☐ Pita bread, whole wheat, pocketless
- ☐ Bagels, whole wheat

CANNED GOODS

- ☐ Garbanzo beans (chickpeas)
- ☐ White beans (butter beans, navy, or cannellini)
- ☐ Refried beans, low-fat, vegetarian
- ☐ Baked beans, vegetarian
- ☐ Tomatoes, plum, whole
- ☐ Sardines, in water, skinless and boneless
- ☐ Tuna, in water (preferably "chunk light")
- ☐ Tomato paste
- ☐ Evaporated skim milk
- ☐ Tomato soup, ideally low-sodium

JARS/BOTTLES

☐ Baby foods—especially sweet potatoes, carrots, peas, zucchini, garden vegetables, prunes, plums, apricots, blueberries, spinach, and broccoli

☐ Pomegranate juice

☐ Salsa

☐ Applesauce

☐ Ranch dressing (no MSG)

☐ Ketchup

☐ Pasta sauce

FROZEN FOODS

☐ Blueberries, (preferably without added syrup or sweeteners)

☐ Strawberries, (preferably without added syrup or sweeteners)

☐ Cherries, (preferably without added syrup or sweeteners)

☐ Green peas, sweet

☐ Corn, yellow, off cob

☐ Edamame (soybeans in shell)

NUTS/OILS

☐ Almonds, blanched and slivered

☐ Walnuts

☐ Extra-virgin olive oil, cold pressed

☐ Canola oil, cold pressed

☐ Cooking oil, spray

TEA/COCOA

☐ Cocoa, unsweetened

☐ Green and herbal teas, decaffeinated

DESSERTS

☐ Chocolate chips, semisweet

☐ Sprinkles, multicolored

☐ Jell-O, not premade

☐ Gelatin, unflavored

☐ Chocolate syrup

☐ Whipped cream, spray can

☐ Frozen yogurt, low-fat

DAIRY/EGGS

☐ Yogurt, low-fat, plain

☐ Cheese, low-fat, shredded

☐ American cheese slices

☐ Ricotta cheese, low-fat

☐ Tofu, firm block

☐ Eggs (with added Omega-3)

☐ Parmesan cheese, grated

☐ Powdered milk, nonfat

OTHER

- [ ] **Chicken broth, boxed (no MSG), ideally low-sodium**
- [ ] **Vegetable broth, boxed, (no MSG), ideally low-sodium**
- [ ] **Cinnamon**
- [ ] **Honey**
- [ ] **Pure maple syrup**
- [ ] **Pure vanilla extract**
- [ ] **Baking powder, non-aluminum**
- [ ] **Baking soda**
- [ ] **Powdered sugar**
- [ ] **Brown sugar**
- [ ] **Jam, no sugar added**
- [ ] **Lentils (dried or canned)**

THE SNEAKY CHEF'S BAG OF TRICKS

As a Sneaky Chef, you will be able to spot the good-for-you twist in the book's recipes, but if you employ the following techniques your kids will be none the wiser—but all that much healthier.

Method One:
PUREE

Pureeing presents food in a concentrated version that makes it extremely nutrient dense, meaning more healthy benefits in every bite. Missy recommends using a blender for smoothies, ice drinks, and soups, since it is better suited to working with liquids or already mushy solids than a food processor. That said, a small food processor has the upper hand when pureeing vegetables, since you don't have to add much, if any, water, which makes for a better, less runny puree. (See page 255 for puree recipes).

Method Two:
COMBINE REFINED AND UNREFINED

This book often calls for a flour blend of one-third white flour, one-third whole-wheat flour, and one-third wheat germ, a ratio that retains a good deal of the usual texture and weight of white flour while also providing the benefit of fiber, vitamins, and minerals.

Method Three:
USE FOODS THAT HIDE WELL

The hallmark of being a Sneaky Chef is the ability to completely hide foods your kids would reject straight-up in foods they'd clean their plate with. The best way to do that is to camouflage the good-for-you ingredient in foods with similar colors and textures. It's crucial, however, that the hidden element either enhances the overall original taste or adds no taste of its own. It's also important that the look or texture isn't changed either. Finally, the golden rule of sneakiness: What you add must be nutritious. Missy's done the hard work to make sure you're a success with even the most picky palettes.

Method Four:
SUBSTITUTE NUTRITIOUS LIQUID FOR WATER WHEN BOILING FOODS

A true Sneaky Chef never misses a trick—or a chance to inject an extra dose of health into a meal. That's why when a job calls for water, consider using a liquid with more nutritional value and a taste that complements the dish, such as chicken or beef broth (providing minerals and protein), veggie broth (potassium, calcium, and minerals), green tea (immunity-building antioxidants), pomegranate or blueberry juice (a day's worth of vitamin C), or low-fat milk (calcium, vitamin D, and protein).

Method Five:
COMBINE FOODS THAT ARE A SPECIFIC NUTRITIONAL COMPLEMENT TO EACH OTHER

If you're having trouble getting your kid to eat one healthy dish, getting them to eat two may seem like a fantasy. The good news is that many of the recipes in this book are designed to combine ingredients that either make a more complete protein or help with the absorption by the body of another nutrient, so you can whip up a single dish that does the nutritional duty of two. Talk about working your magic in the kitchen!

Method Six:
IDENTIFY FOODS KIDS ARE LIKELY TO ENJOY STRAIGHT-UP

Why make your life hard when it doesn't have to be? It may be difficult to believe during a stand-off at the dinner table, but there are actually good-for-you foods that kids *will* eat without a fight. Offer them snacks like edamame (soybeans), cherries, snap peas, strawberries, corn on the cob, pistachios, sunflower seeds, baby carrots, popcorn, artichokes, whole grapes, roasted chestnuts, and even hummus. Keep in mind that the foods will be more appealing if your child is hungry and if there isn't any junk food around to tempt them. You'll also get better results if they're distracted, if they're with kids their age who'll eat the food without a fuss, or if you're spotted enjoying them—and don't offer to share.

Method Seven:

ALTER THE COOKING METHOD TO AVOID FRYING

Steam, bake, broil, roast, or grill instead of frying. Putting away your deep fryer doesn't mean you have to shelve flavor—or a satisfying crunch. Use these methods to make the most of the oils you employ: measuring the oil with a teaspoon instead of pouring it right out of the bottle, using a pastry brush to baste the oil on, blasting the dish with high heat under the broiler for a minute to crisp the breading, and swapping juice or broth for oil, all work to give a recipe the moistness a fried food would have.

Method Eight:

CUT THE EFFECT OF TOXINS OR FATS BY DILUTING THE INGREDIENTS WITH SOMETHING HEALTHIER

You'll never get your kid to give up on unhealthy treats entirely (and what's the fun in that anyway?). So let them eat cake (or whatever it is that they crave) but reduce the "junk" factor by diluting it with something healthy. For example, reduce the mercury levels in his favorite tuna fish sandwich by diluting it with heart-healthy sardines; mix plain yogurt into high-fat creamy salad dressings; substitute fruit, vegetable, or bean puree for butter in baked goods; cut fruit juice with decaffeinated green tea or water; thicken sauces and soups with bean puree. Just be sure that whatever you add doesn't dilute the original taste, and both you and your child will have a truly happy meal.

CUT CALORIES AND DOUBLE VOLUME WITH LOW-CAL, NUTRITIOUS "FILLERS"

"Fill 'em up" has an all-new meaning: by adding volume with nutritious ingredients that have fewer calories per portion, such as mixing veggies into your meatballs or pureed cauliflower into your mashed potatoes, you'll feel more satisfied with fewer calories. Bulking up works best with ingredients that have a high water and fiber content, like fruits and veggies.

USE SLOWER BURNING FOODS TO AVOID BLOOD SUGAR "SPIKE AND CRASH"

Ever give your child a handful of jellybeans only to see them bounce off the walls before sinking into an overtired meltdown? That's the sugar at work. Refined-sugar foods and and carbohydrates like white bread and pastas make your blood sugar shoot up, and may give you a quick burst of energy. But soon after, your blood sugar tends to plummet, leaving you feeling lethargic and even hungrier than before. Complex carbs like whole grains and proteins like beans and legumes, however, take longer to digest and therefore keep your blood sugar, appetite, and energy level steady.

Method Eleven:
USE VISUAL DECOYS TO MAKE FOOD LOOK APPEALING AND FUN

If kids can't see the healthy food, they'll eat it, so make use of appealing colors, fun shapes, and surprising sizes to divert their attention from what's really on their plate. Dust powdered sugar on baked goods, serve foods in mini-sizes or in individual containers like muffin liners, shape food with cookie cutters, let them "play" with their food by making them "dip-able."

Method Twelve:
USE KID-FRIENDLY FLAVOR DECOYS TO DISTRACT KIDS FROM WHAT'S UNDERNEATH

All your efforts will go for naught if the taste of something suspicious pulls back the curtain on you, so make the most of bold flavors that kids love. Include flavors that are strong enough to cover up your covert ops, like cheese, cocoa, chocolate chips, marshmallows, ranch dressing, and, maybe the most valuable decoy in your kitchen, ketchup.

Method Thirteen:

USE KID-FRIENDLY TEXTURE DECOYS

In their own way, kids are connoisseurs. Something may look and taste great, but should they detect anything lumpy, gritty, or leafy, their noses will turn up like a gourmand at a drive-thru window. If you're worried that a texture will be objectionable to your child, add a decoy texture that they'll approve of: Sprinkles, chocolate chips, cheese, crushed cereal toppings, and raisins are sure to get a four-star review.

NEED A BOOST? CALL FOR A SUPERFOOD!

Like a superhero, these foods can pack a wallop (of nutrition) into simple, everyday dishes. Missy turns to them time and time again for her good-for-you recipes, but you can include them in your favorite meals whenever you're looking for a healthy helping hand.

ALMONDS

A snack with staying power, a one-ounce serving of almonds is packed with vitamin E, magnesium, fiber, phosphorous. monounsaturated fat, protein, potassium, calcium, and iron—all of which team up to lower your risk for heart disease.

BANANAS

Easy to eat on the go, bananas are high in potassium, fiber, vitamin B6 and manganese and are low in saturated fat, cholesterol, and sodium. Bananas keep your heart healthy, aid digestion and shore up your eyes and bones.

BLUEBERRIES

They may be tiny, but these baby blues are one of the most powerful antioxidants; they help to ward off diseases such as cancer and cardiovascular disease and are a natural brain-booster!

BROCCOLI

No wonder mothers everywhere have begged their kids to eat their broccoli—it's high in protein, fiber, calcium, and vitamin C and may guard against many different types of cancers.

CARROTS

These crunchy veggies are one of the richest sources of pro-vitamin A carotenes, which promote healthy hearts and keep your eyes sharp.

CAULIFLOWER

It may look bland, but this white veggie comes with folate, fiber, and vitamin C, which help keep cancer, rheumatoid arthritis, and cardiovascular and other diseases at bay.

CHERRIES

With tons of antioxidants, beta carotene, vitamin C, potassium, magnesium, iron, fiber, and folate, these ruby reds can reduce pain and inflammation and lower your risk for heart disease, diabetes, and some cancers. They may even help you sleep better, too.

CHICKPEAS

Also known as garbanzo beans, chickpeas are high in fiber, folate, tryptophan, magnesium, and iron, protecting your heart and giving you an energy boost. When they're paired with simple carbs, they help keep your blood sugars steady.

GREEN PEAS

Small but mighty, these legumes boast a boatload of vitamin K, which keeps your bones healthy. Fiber, vitamin C, and potassium come along for the ride, meaning your heart will be looked after, as well.

LENTILS

High in fiber, iron, protein, magnesium, and folate, lentils give you a big bang for your buck by keeping you feeling full and energized, lowering your risk of heart disease, and maintaining a healthy digestive track.

SPINACH

Talk about pumping iron—spinach gives you twice as much as any other leafy green, and also has calcium, folic acid, vitamins A and C, and beta-carotene. Spinach builds strong bones, keeps your eyes and brain in focus, and protects against asthma, arthritis, cancer, and heart disease. No wonder Popeye's a fan.

STRAWBERRIES

A serving of these sweet berries give you as much vitamin C as an orange and is a great source of folic acid, fiber, potassium, and antioxidants. Strawberries keep your brain and heart healthy and help ward off cancer.

SWEET POTATOES AND YAMS

You may not want to limit these sweet spuds to your Thanksgiving table. Their high levels of complex carbohydrates, fiber, B vitamins, folate, antioxidants, carotenes, calcium, potassium, and iron keep blood sugars even, boost moods, and make sleep easier *all* year round.

WHEAT GERM

With plenty of iron, protein, B vitamins, folic acid, vitamin E, zinc, magnesium, manganese, and chromium, wheat germ supports your nervous system and keeps fatigue from running you down.

WHITE BEANS

Like other legumes, these beans will keep your blood sugar steady and form a complete protein when paired with grains or rice. They also have heaps of folate, trytophan, magnesium, and iron, which give your brain a boost and protect against cancer and heart disease.

WHOLE-WHEAT FLOUR

Manganese, magnesium, trytophan, and fiber make whole-wheat flour a powerful addition to any recipe. It helps to regulate digestion and keeps your blood sugar at an even keel.

ZUCCHINI

Last but far from least, this squash comes with a helping of fiber, manganese, vitamin C, and potassium to help keep asthma, some cancers, and heart disease at arm's length.

The Sneaky Fitness Recipes

Now you're ready to start cooking! Just a few notes before we begin:

1. For each recipe, the sneaky ingredients are highlighted in gray.

2. All the recipes can be frozen for up to three months and kept in the refrigerator for three days.

3. All recipes for the make-ahead purees can be found in Chapter 7, starting on page 255.

4. The truly skillful Sneaky Chef sneaks up on the family with these methods.

That is to say, a Sneaky Chef uses only a small amount of the Sneaky puree for the first few times. Then gradually increase the amount of the puree, adding only as much as you can get away with.

4. Cooking spray is often called for in the recipes. Use an additive-free, natural olive oil or canola oil spray or mist, or make your own by putting the healthy oil of your choice into a spray bottle.

6. You'll notice icons at the top of each recipe. They indicate the nutrition highlights, and are a quick way to tell if the recipe fits your goals:

 Whole Grains: includes a healthy amount of whole grains

 Veggie: vegetarian recipe (may include eggs and dairy, but no fish, poultry, or meat)

 Antioxidant Boost: contains a number of antioxidants

 Protein Boost: contains a good amount of protein

 Low Sugar: contains no added sugar or sweeteners

 Healthy Fats: contains heart healthy (monounsaturated) fats, like olive or nut oils, avocado, or nuts

Have fun!

Clever Crepes

Crepes are very thin pancakes, traditionally folded and filled with sweet or savory ingredients. Missy serves the sweet versions below for breakfast—kids think they're getting a treat, but you'll know there's some nutrition slipped in. Best of all, you can make them ahead, then refrigerate or freeze for later. On a busy weekday morning, all you have to do is grab 'em, fill 'em, and go! Wrap them in wax paper like they do on the streets of Paris, and your kids will say "ooo la la!"

MAKES ABOUT 4 CREPES

1 large egg

1 large egg white
(about 3 tablespoons
liquid egg white)

¾ cup low-fat milk

1 tablespoon sugar

¼ teaspoon salt

½ cup Flour Blend
(see Make-Ahead
Recipe #8, p. 265)

In a large mixing bowl, whisk together all the ingredients until smooth. Unlike pancakes, you don't want any lumps in crepe batter.

Heat a small (about 8-inch) nonstick frying pan over medium-high heat. Coat the entire bottom and sides of the pan generously with cooking spray oil.

Pour about ¼ cup of batter into the hot pan. Lift and tilt the pan to swirl the batter so that it covers the bottom of the pan evenly, with no pools of batter remaining. Cook the crepe for about one minute, until the top is no longer wet and the edges start to brown. Loosen edges with a rubber-tipped spatula, flip, and cook the other side for another minute.

Repeat with remaining batter, re-spraying the pan before making each crepe. If serving immediately, see variations below and fill each crepe in the pan. Or, crepes can be made in advance, stacked between sheets of wax paper wrapped in plastic, and stored refrigerated for 3 days or frozen for 3 months (thaw before using).

PER SERVING (1 CREPE, 100G): *Calories 156; Total Fat 4g; Fiber 3g; Total Carbohydrate 22g; Sugars 3g; Protein 9g; Sodium 206mg; Cholesterol 157mg; Calcium 70mg*

Breakfast Crepe Fillings:

Put 1 tablespoon Peanut Butter or Nutella® mixed with ½ tablespoon Orange Puree (see Make-Ahead Recipe #2, p. 258) in the center of the crepe; add banana (optional), fold in quarters, and dust with powdered sugar.

Put 1 tablespoon jam mixed with 1 teaspoon ground flax seeds in the center of the crepe; add sliced strawberries or raspberries (optional), fold in quarters, and dust with powdered sugar.

Put 1 tablespoon chocolate syrup with sliced bananas in the center of the crepe, fold in quarters, and dust with powdered sugar.

**BREAKFAST
PAN PIZZA**

*Sneaky
Ingredients:*
Cauliflower,
Zucchini,
Whole Wheat,
Tomato Paste

**TOP DOG
CORN
MUFFINS**

*Sneaky
Ingredients:*
Cauliflower,
Zucchini,
Whole Wheat

CHOCOLATE CHAMPION CEREAL COOKIES

Sneaky Ingredients: Spinach, Blueberries, Oats, Whole Wheat

HOT DOGGITOS

Sneaky Ingredients: Cauliflower, Zucchini, Whole Wheat

SURPRISE-ICLES

Sneaky Ingredients:
Carrots,
Sweet Potatoes,
Yogurt

HONEY BBQ CHICKEN NUGGETS

Sneaky Ingredients:
Blueberries,
Spinach,
Flax,
Wheat Germ

**CHOCOLATE
NO-ACHE SHAKE**

Sneaky Ingredients:
Bananas,
Cherries

**OFF-THE-COUCH
POTATO SKINS**

Sneaky Ingredients
Cauliflower,
Zucchini,
Yogurt

**CHICKEN
PARMESAN
PANINI**

*Sneaky
Ingredients:*
Cauliflower,
Flax,
Tomato Paste,
Wheat Germ,
Zucchini

RAINBOW PANCAKES

Sneaky Ingredients:
Oats,
Whole Wheat,
Cottage Cheese

MAKE MINE A MAC N CHEESE PIZZA

Sneaky Ingredients:
Whole Wheat,
Cauliflower,
Zucchini,
Carrots,
Sweet Potatoes

**SUPER-
CHARGED
TUNA SLIDERS**

Sneaky

Ingredients:

White Beans,

Wheat Germ

**CRUNCHY
CHOCOLATE
CLUSTERS**

Sneaky

Ingredients:

Oats,

Oat Bran,

Flax,

Walnuts

**CHEESE
FUN-DO**

*Sneaky
Ingredients:*
Apple Juice
Cauliflower,
Zucchini

**SNEAKY
S'MORES**

*Sneaky
Ingredients:*
Carrots,
Sweet Potatoes,
Oats,
Whole Wheat

BLUE RIBBON ICE CREAM SANDWICHES *Sneaky Ingredients:* Blueberries, Ricotta Cheese
BLACK FOREST CUPCAKES *Sneaky Ingredients:* Pomegranate Juice, Cherries, Wheat Germ
SNEAKY STRAWBERRY CUPCAKES *Sneaky Ingredients:* Cranberry Juice, Oat Bran, Strawberries

Go-Go Granola

What a way to start the day: fiber, protein, good fats, and great crunch! A little of this easy-to-make granola goes a long way since it's packed with a protein/fiber combo that satisfies hunger and keeps blood sugar steady. A true power breakfast, the long energy burn will keep your kids on the go all morning. Pair it with milk for a yummy boost of calcium and protein.

MAKES 4 CUPS (12 SERVINGS)

2 cups rolled oats

1 cup ground almonds (see Make-Ahead Recipe #9, p. 266)

¼ cup oat bran

¼ cup ground flax seeds

1 teaspoon each salt

1 teaspoon cinnamon

4 tablespoons canola or almond oil

½ cup honey

Toast almonds and oats in a large 10- to 12-inch dry skillet over medium-low heat, stirring occasionally until lightly browned, about 5 minutes (reduce heat if starting to burn). Meanwhile mix the oat bran, flax, salt, and cinnamon in a large mixing bowl. Add the warm, toasted almonds and oats to the mixing bowl and stir to combine. Wipe skillet with a paper towel, return it to the stovetop, and reduce heat to low. Add the oil and honey, stirring until melted and foaming, about 1 minute. Pour the hot mixture into the mixing bowl and quickly toss to coat all ingredients.

Allow granola to cool in the bowl. When cool enough to handle, occasionally squeeze together clumps of granola with your fingers (or roll into small balls with oiled hands). This will help form crunchy clusters.

Store in an airtight container in the refrigerator for up to one week, or in the freezer for up to 3 months.

Serve with milk as cereal or eat as a dry, handheld snack.

Note: Be sure to refrigerate flax after it's been ground to retain freshness.

PER SERVING (⅓ CUP, 70G): *Calories 255; Total Fat 12g; Fiber 5g; Total Carbohydrate 33g; Sugars 12g; Protein 7g; Sodium 220mg; Cholesterol 0mg; Calcium 50mg*

Get a Move on Muffin Soufflés

Sometimes all it takes to make a food appeal to a kid is to change the shape or serving method. Think animal crackers versus tea biscuits. They both have the same ingredients, but chances are your kids will gobble up the cute animal shapes before the boring rectangles! Likewise, kids may turn their noses up when offered quiche or soufflé, but turn them into a wholesome, portable kid-friendly egg muffin and watch how fast they reach for one. The bread gives it structure and whole-grain goodness. You can use any sausage, bacon, or ham and a favorite cheese for flavor decoys. Prep them the night before, pop them in the oven while getting dressed in the morning, and you'll have a full one-dish family breakfast ready and waiting. Plus: no dishes to wash!

MAKES 6 SERVINGS

½ cup shredded low-fat cheddar or
    Colby cheese, divided

2 large eggs

1 egg white (or 3 tablespoons liquid
    egg white)

¾ cup evaporated skim milk

¼ cup Orange Puree (see Make-Ahead #2,
    page 258)

2 slices cooked bacon, roughly chopped

½ thin baguette or French bread, ideally
    whole grain, sliced

Preheat oven to 375 degrees and grease or spray nonstick muffin tins.

In mixing bowl, whisk the eggs, egg white, evaporated skim milk, and Orange Puree. Mix in bacon and ¼ cup of the cheese.

Place a small slice of bread in each muffin cup. Pour about ¼ cup of egg mixture into each cup, filling almost to the top. Top evenly with the remaining cheese. Bake for 20 to 25 minutes until eggs are set and cheese is lightly browned and bubbly.

PER SERVING (1 SOUFFLE, 82 G): *Calories 109; Total Fat 4g; Fiber 1g; Total Carbohydrate 9g; Sugars 5g; Protein 10g; Sodium 226mg; Cholesterol 77mg; Calcium 150mg*

Sneaky *Time-Saving* Tip!

Missy often cooks a package of bacon on Sunday morning, then leaves it wrapped in paper towels inside a sealed plastic bag in the fridge for use during the week.

Jumping Jelly Omelet

An old-fashioned omelet filled with jelly, with a delicious and nutritious twist. Roll it up in a whole-grain tortilla and parchment, and you'll have a hand-held take-anywhere breakfast.

MAKES 1 SERVING

1 teaspoon butter

1 large egg

2 tablespoons Orange Puree (see Make-Ahead #2, page 258), divided

1 teaspoon ground flax seeds

1 tablespoon jam

1 flour tortilla, ideally whole grain

Pinch of salt

Pinch of sugar

Melt butter in a small nonstick skillet over medium heat. Crack the egg into a mixing bowl and whisk in one tablespoon of the Orange Puree until well incorporated. Add the beaten egg mixture to the skillet, allow to set briefly, and then, using a rubber spatula, lift edges of eggs as they cook, letting uncooked part run underneath until omelet is completely set. While the egg is cooking, mix the ground flax and remaining Orange Puree into the jam in a small mixing bowl. Spoon the jam mixture onto the middle of the fully cooked omelet in the pan, spread it slightly, then fold omelet in half. Remove omelet from pan and lay on the bottom half of a warm tortilla, season with a pinch of salt and sugar, then roll up to create a cigar shape.

PER SERVING (1 OMELET, 134G): *Calories 265; Total Fat 12g; Fiber 3g; Total Carbohydrate 30g; Sugar 12g; Protein 9g; Sodium 199mg; Cholesterol 222mg; Calcium 80mg*

Cinnamon Toast Warm-Up

veggie · healthy fats · whole grains

What better way to coax your kids to eat flax than with the aroma of cinnamon? This simple recipe is how Missy first introduced her children to flax. The cinnamon sugar completely disguised the look and taste of omega-3 rich flax. She especially loves getting flax into kids in the morning before school because it's high in fiber, which keeps them full, and has tons of essential fatty acids that boost their brain power.

MAKES 2 SERVINGS

1 tablespoon ground
    flax seeds

2 teaspoons sugar,
    ideally raw

¼ teaspoon ground
    cinnamon

2 slices cinnamon-raisin
    bread, ideally whole
    grain

2 teaspoons unsalted
    butter, room temp

In a small bowl, mix the flax, sugar, and cinnamon.

Toast the bread until golden, then butter and sprinkle generously with the cinnamon-sugar mixture. Serve warm.

PER SERVING (1 SLICE, 41G): *Calories 156; Total Fat 12g; Fiber 3g; Total Carbohydrate 18g; Sugar 6g; Protein 5g; Sodium 113mg; Cholesterol 4mg; Calcium 50mg*

Toast 'n' jam variation:

Substitute 1 tablespoon favorite jam for the cinnamon and sugar above, mixing the flax into the jam and spreading on buttered toast.

Breakfast "Sushi"

Finger food for breakfast! Once again, it's all in the delivery. This recipe transforms a boring ol' sandwich into an exotic hand-held treat. The flattened crustless bread stands in for "seaweed" and wraps around the good-for-you cheese, puree, and bacon filling. Roll it up, slice, and serve. (Chopsticks optional!)

MAKES 2 SERVINGS

2 slices bread, ideally whole grain

2 tablespoons Orange Puree (see Make-Ahead #2, page 258), divided

2 slices American cheese

2 slices cooked **turkey bacon or Canadian bacon**

Preheat oven (or toaster oven) to 350 degrees.

Trim crust off bread. Use a rolling pin to roll out each slice of bread on a cutting board until flattened (alternatively, use the palm of your hand to flatten the bread). Spread about 1 tablespoon of Orange Puree on each flattened slice of bread, keeping about ¼ inch away from the edges. Lay a slice of cheese on top of the puree on each slice of bread, then lay a slice of cooked bacon on top of each slice of cheese.

Roll up and insert a few toothpicks to hold the roll closed. Bake for 8 to 10 minutes, until bread is lightly toasted and cheese is melted. Slice each roll into 3 pieces and serve.

PER SERVING (45G): *Calories 244; Total Fat 8g; Fiber 4g; Total Carbohydrate 25g; Sugar 0g; Protein 11g; Sodium 648mg; Cholesterol 32mg; Calcium 152mg*

Chocolate Champion Cereal Cookies

Offer cookies for breakfast, and you've already won the World's Greatest Mom contest! These rich, chocolate cookies have less sugar and more whole grains than most kids' breakfast cereals. Plus, they come with a hidden "prize" of their own: spinach and blueberries. Make a few batches and freeze so all you have to do is reach for a couple on rushed weekday mornings. Dust lightly with powdered sugar just before serving for added kid appeal.

MAKES 3 DOZEN COOKIES

½ cup rolled oats

½ **cup Flour Blend (see Make-Ahead Recipe #8, p. 265)**

3 cups whole-grain cereal flakes, such as Wheaties® or Total®

¼ cup cocoa

½ teaspoon baking soda

1 large egg

⅓ **cup Purple Puree (see Make-Ahead Recipe #1, p. 257)**

¾ cup sugar

1 teaspoon pure vanilla extract

6 tablespoons unsalted butter, softened

Preheat the oven to 350 degrees and line a baking sheet with parchment paper.

Place the oats in the bowl of a food processor and process on high until oats are finely ground. Add the cereal flakes and pulse several times until the flakes resemble crumbs. Transfer processed oats and cereal to a large mixing bowl and whisk in the Flour Blend, cocoa, and baking soda. In another bowl, whisk together egg, Purple Puree, sugar, vanilla, and cooled softened butter. Add the dry ingredients to the wet and mix just until combined. Drop single tablespoonfuls of batter onto the baking sheets, leaving about an inch between each cookie. Flatten the cookies with the back of a fork that's been sprayed with oil to keep from sticking to the batter. Bake 12 to 15 minutes, until lightly browned around the edges.

Remove from the pan and let cool. Store in an airtight container or freeze in sealed plastic bags for up to 3 months.

PER SERVING (SERVING SIZE 1 COOKIE, 16G):
Calories 59; Total Fat 2g; Fiber 1g; Total Carbohydrate 9g; Sugar 5g; Protein 1g; Sodium 41mg; Cholesterol 8mg; Calcium 110mg

Rainbow Pancakes with Warm Strawberry Syrup

*Who among us can get our kids to eat cottage cheese and wheat germ in the morning (okay, make that any time of the day)? Now we can! All it takes is using The Sneaky Chef "Decoy" method. Kids will eat anything with sprinkles on top, but they'll also eat things with sprinkles **inside**—even if there's also lots of good-for-you ingredients in there too.*

MAKES 36 SILVER DOLLARS (ABOUT 6 SERVINGS)

½ cup low-fat cottage cheese

½ cup low-fat milk

1 teaspoon pure vanilla extract

1 large egg

½ cup rolled oats

¼ teaspoon salt

1 teaspoon baking powder

½ cup Flour Blend (see Make-Ahead
    Recipe #8, p. 265)

1 tablespoon multi-colored sprinkles

Strawberry syrup (next page)

Powdered sugar, optional

In the container of a blender, combine all ingredients except Flour Blend and sprinkles and blend until smooth. Add Flour Blend and pulse a few times until the dry ingredients are fully incorporated. *Add the sprinkles and mix lightly with a spoon (do not blend the sprinkles—you want them to remain whole).*

Spray non-stick cooking oil on a griddle or large skillet over medium heat. Test the pan by tossing in a few drops of water; it will sizzle when it's hot enough. The skillet will grow hotter over time, so turn down the heat if the pan starts to smoke.

Drop small ladles (about 1 tablespoon) of batter onto the skillet in batches, making sure there are some sprinkles in each pancake. Pancakes should be small—about 1½ inches across in size. When bubbles begin to set around the edges and the skillet-side of each pancake is golden (peek underneath), gently flip them over. Continue to cook 2 to 3 minutes or until the pancake is fully set.

Serve stacked high, drizzled with a little warm Strawberry Syrup (see recipe below) or dusted with powdered sugar.

PER SERVING (6 SILVER DOLLARS, 83G): *Calories 155; Total Fat 3g; Fiber 3g; Total Carbohydrate 24g; Sugar 2g; Protein 9g; Sodium 196mg; Cholesterol 37mg; Calcium 90mg*

Strawberry Syrup:

Strawberry Puree (see Make-Ahead Recipe #5, p. 262) combined with an equal part pure maple syrup. Warm, and serve.

Sneaky
Time-Saving Tip!

Put all ingredients (except the sprinkles) in the blender the night before and refrigerate overnight. You can also make extra pancakes on leisurely Sunday mornings and simply reheat and serve for the next few days.

Muscle Man Maple Sausage Griddle Cakes

Who says sausage has to go alongside the pancake? It's a whole lot yummier to put it right inside! This fun, savory breakfast griddle cake boasts flavor and protein. Is your kid always on the go? Make them ahead, freeze for up to 3 months, and just pop them in the toaster in the morning.

MAKES ABOUT 2 DOZEN (APPROXIMATELY 8 SERVINGS)

4 breakfast sausages, ideally chicken maple flavor, sliced into small pieces

1 large egg

¼ **cup Orange Puree (see Make-Ahead Recipe #2, p. 258)**

½ cup low-fat milk

3 tablespoons pure maple syrup

1 teaspoon pure vanilla extract

½ **cup Flour Blend (see Make-Ahead Recipe #8, p. 265)**

2 teaspoons baking powder

¼ teaspoon salt

Maple syrup, for serving

Butter or spray a large skillet or griddle over medium heat. Brown the sausages evenly, then remove, set aside, and wipe out the skillet. In a large bowl, whisk together the egg, Orange Puree, milk, maple syrup, and vanilla. In another bowl, whisk together the Flour Blend, baking powder, and salt.

Stir the wet ingredients into the dry until just blended. Batter should be fairly thick and slightly lumpy. If the batter is too thick, add a touch more milk. Add the sausage, and mix lightly.

Butter or spray the griddle or skillet over medium heat. Test the pan by tossing in a few drops of water; it will sizzle when it's hot enough. The skillet will grow hotter over time, so turn down the heat if the pan starts to smoke.

Drop medium-size ladles of batter onto the skillet in batches (aiming for approximately 3-inch pancakes), making sure there is some sausage in each pancake. When bubbles begin to set around the edges and the skillet-side of each pancake is golden (peek underneath), gently flip them over. Continue to cook 2 to 3 minutes or until the pancake is fully set.

Serve stacked high, drizzled with a little more maple syrup.

PER SERVING (3 GRIDDLE CAKES, 65G): *Calories 124; Total Fat 4g; Fiber 2g; Total Carbohydrate 17g; Sugar 6g; Protein 6g; Sodium 177mg; Cholesterol 50mg; Calcium 90mg*

Q: What can I put in my kid's lunchbox beyond sandwiches? I'm getting bored making the same thing over and over—I can only imagine how he feels having to eat it. Help!

A: It's easier than you think to move away from the breadbox. Turn to muffin tins, for example. Missy's Lunch Box Muffin has become popular as a fun, hand-held full meal alternative to sandwiches. (Find the recipe at TheSneakyChef.com.) Also, many kids love to take leftover pancakes for lunch (even cold), so try the Muscle Man Maple Sausage Griddle Cakes. They're full of whole grains and protein and will keep your child feeling full of energy until the last school bell rings.

Breakfast Pan Pizza

Some kids just won't touch an egg with a 10-foot pole, but pizza is rarely turned down. So transform an omelet or scrambled eggs into a yummy breakfast pizza. The whole-grain tortilla at the bottom of the pan provides an instant crust.

Prep all the ingredients in a mixing bowl the night before, leave in the fridge, and pour into the pan in the morning. The bubbling hot cheese topping gives this dish great eye appeal. Plus, ketchup not only acts as pizza sauce, but it also gives you another good hiding place for veggie puree. Shhh!

MAKES 6 TO 8 SERVINGS

4 large eggs

4 egg whites (or ¾ cup liquid egg whites)

2 tablespoons low-fat milk

½ cup plus 1 tablespoon White Puree (see Make-Ahead Recipe #4, p. 260), divided

2 cups shredded low-fat cheddar cheese, divided

1 cup Canadian or turkey bacon, diced, optional

1 tablespoon butter

1 whole-wheat flour tortilla (10- to 12-inch)

2 tablespoons ketchup or tomato paste

Salt and freshly ground pepper, to taste

Preheat oven to 425 degrees.

In a large bowl, whisk together eggs, egg whites, milk, ½ cup of the White Puree, ½ cup of the cheese, and bacon, if using.

Melt butter in a large (10- to 12-inch) oven-proof skillet over medium heat. Add the tortilla and heat for 1 minute, then flip and cook for another minute. Pour the egg mixture into the skillet over the tortilla.

Let the egg mixture set without stirring. Meanwhile, mix the ketchup with remaining tablespoon White Puree. When the pan pizza is almost fully set, lightly spoon on ketchup mixture, then top with the remaining 1 and ½ cups of cheese.

Transfer the pan to the heated oven. Bake for 10 minutes until puffed and golden. Slice and serve.

PER SERVING (1 SLICE, 103G): *Calories 141; Total Fat 7g; Fiber 1g; Total Carbohydrate 7g; Sugar 2g; Protein 13g; Sodium 337mg; Cholesterol 116mg; Calcium 150mg(1 slice, 103g): Calories 141; Total Fat 7g; Fiber 1g; Total Carbohydrate 7g; Sugar 2g; Protein 13g; Sodium 337mg; Cholesterol 116mg; Calcium 150mg*

Phabulous Philly Cheesesteak

The cheesesteak is a well-known Philadelphia delicacy, but is less known as being part of a healthy diet. Until now, that is. Traditionally made with very thinly-shaved steak, Missy swapped it for ground beef in order to slip in her veggie puree. Personalize yours, Philly-style, "wit" or "witout" grilled onions and peppers.

MAKES 4 SERVINGS

1 tablespoon olive oil

1 medium onion, halved and sliced thin, optional

1 bell pepper, sliced thin, optional

1 pound lean ground beef

6 tablespoons ketchup

¼ cup Green Puree (see Make-Ahead Recipe #3, p. 259)

Salt and freshly ground pepper, to taste

4 soft Italian hoagie rolls, ideally whole grain

For easy cheesy sauce:

4 slices American or Provolone cheese

3 tablespoons Orange or White Puree (see Make-Ahead Recipes #2, p. 258; #4, p. 260).

Heat the oil over medium heat in a nonstick skillet. Add the onion and pepper, if using, and cook until they are lightly browned, about 10 minutes. Remove from skillet and set aside, cover, and keep warm. Add the ground beef, stirring to break it up, and cook for about 5 minutes, until the meat is no longer red. Meanwhile, in a mixing bowl, combine the ketchup with the Green Puree until the mixture turns brownish. Stir the ketchup mixture into the beef in the skillet, and mix well.

To make the cheese sauce:

Combine cheese and Orange or White Puree in a microwave-safe bowl. Cover the top of the bowl with a wet paper towel and microwave on high for 30 seconds at a time until fully melted.

Assemble sandwiches:

Hollow out a little of the soft inner part of each roll to make room for filling. Divide meat equally among the rolls and top with onions, peppers, and cheese sauce, if using. Season with salt and pepper, to taste. Wrap each sandwich individually in aluminum foil and keep warm until ready to serve (serve in foil for extra authentic feel).

PER SERVING (1 SANDWICH, 223G): *Calories 422; Total Fat 19g; Fiber 2g; Total Carbohydrate 27g; Sugar 8g; Protein 36g; Sodium 770mg; Cholesterol 89mg; Calcium 270mg*

Intro to Hummus

protein boost   anti oxidant boost   veggie

As your kids grow into tweens, their palate grows too—though some kids need to be introduced to stronger flavors more slowly than others. That's why Missy included the familiar, lovable taste of peanut butter and honey to replace the sesame paste and garlic traditionally used in more sophisticated hummus. Kids of all ages love to dip, so surround the hummus bowl with your child's favorite dippers like whole-grain pita chips, crunchy cucumber rounds, or carrots. The combination of whole grains, beans, veggies, and good fats make this a substantial after-school mini-meal.

MAKES 4 SERVINGS

¼ cup creamy peanut butter

5 tablespoons White Puree

(see Make-Ahead Recipe #4, p. 260)

1 cup canned chickpeas, drained and rinsed

2 tablespoons freshly squeezed lemon juice

½ teaspoon salt

2 teaspoons honey

4 teaspoons water

Dippers: Toasted whole-grain pita triangles
   or chips, cucumber rounds, and/or
   carrot sticks.

Place all the ingredients in the bowl of a food processor and puree on high, stopping occasionally to scrape the sides of the bowl until mixture is a very smooth dip.

PER SERVING (76G): *Calories 176; Total Fat 9g; Fiber 4g; Total Carbohydrate 18g; Sugar 7g; Protein 8g; Sodium 369mg; Cholesterol 0mg; Calcium 30mg*

Chicken Noodle Salad

Like chicken noodle soup, this is a kid-pleaser and makes a nice "intro to salad" for the tween set. Missy has chosen very basic, sweet, salad veggies so your kid won't be tempted to wrinkle his or her nose at an unknown food, and the noodles are a fun incentive to keep eating! The real key to this salad's success, however, is to dice all the components in small and equal sizes, which gives each forkful a crunchy mixture of all the ingredients. The sneak? It's in the dressing, but we're not telling!

MAKES 4 SERVINGS

2 carrots, diced

2 stalks celery, diced

1 red bell pepper, diced

2 cups small pasta noodles, like small shells
  or elbows, cooked

2 cups cooked chicken, diced

3 cups romaine lettuce, chopped small

Optional: handful of chopped fresh dill
  or parsley, grape tomatoes, and/or
  grated parmesan cheese

PER SERVING (252G): *Calories 225; Total Fat 3g; Fiber 3g; Total Carbohydrate 23g; Sugar 3g; Protein 25g; Sodium 89mg; Cholesterol 76mg; Calcium 40mg*

BBQ Ranch Dressing:

MAKES 6 TABLESPOONS

**2 tablespoons White Puree
  (see Make-Ahead Recipe #4, p. 260)**

4 tablespoons low-fat ranch dressing

2 tablespoons apple cider vinegar or
  red wine vinegar

2 tablespoons store-bought BBQ sauce

OR

Honey Mustard Vinaigrette:

MAKES 6 TABLESPOONS

2 tablespoons White Puree

  (see Make-Ahead Recipe #4, p. 260)

2 teaspoons honey or non-spicy mustard

2 teaspoons honey

2 tablespoons apple cider vinegar

2 tablespoons extra-virgin olive oil

Whisk the dressing ingredients together. Using tongs and a large mixing bowl, toss salad ingredients with dressing to coat well.

Beefed-Up Barley Soup

protein boost · healthy fats · anti oxidant boost · low sugar

Most kids love this classic soup. And why not? It's rich and hearty and is a full-course meal in a single bowl. Missy has snuck in Green Puree and tomato paste, but you can puree up any cooked veggie you want to hide—carrots, onions, and mushrooms all work well here, too.

MAKES 6 TO 8 SERVINGS

2 tablespoons extra-virgin olive oil

1 medium onion, diced

2 stalks celery, diced

1 to 2 garlic cloves, minced

½ pound lean ground beef

¼ cup Green Puree (see Make-Ahead Recipe #3, p. 259)

1 (6-ounce) can tomato paste

1 teaspoon dried oregano

4 cups store-bought beef broth

½ cup pearl barley, uncooked*

Salt and freshly ground pepper, to taste

PER SERVING (284G): *Calories 191; Total Fat 7g; Fiber 5g; Total Carbohydrate 22g; Sugar 5g; Protein 12g; Sodium 483mg; Cholesterol 23mg; Calcium 40mg*

Heat the oil over medium heat in a large soup pot. Add the onion and cook until slightly translucent, about 5 minutes; add the celery and garlic, and sauté for another 5 minutes. Add the ground beef, stirring to break up the meat, and cook for about 10 minutes, until the meat is no longer red.

In a mixing bowl, combine the Green Puree and tomato paste until the mixture turns brownish in color, and stir into meat mixture in pot. Add the oregano, broth, and barley, bring to a boil, and then reduce heat to low, cover, and gently simmer for 30 to 45 minutes or until barley is tender.*

Ladle the soup into bowls and season with salt and freshly ground pepper, to taste.

To save time, use "quick-cooking barley" and simmer soup for just 10 to 15 minutes until barley is tender.

Top Dog Corn Muffins

While giving a radio interview in Minneapolis, Missy was challenged to take corndogs, their favorite county fair fare, and remake them healthier at home. The first thing she threw out was the deep-frying— even a Sneaky Chef can't make healthy out of that. But once she transformed corn dogs into muffins, she could sneak in whole grains, veggies, and calcium while retaining the traditional great taste of hot dogs and cornbread. This complete meal in a muffin makes a fun dinner on the run or lunchbox sandwich alternative.

This recipe is not advised for kids under 3, as hot dogs can pose a choking hazard.

MAKES 8 MUFFINS

1 large egg

2 tablespoons sugar

2 tablespoons butter, melted

½ cup White Puree (See Make-Ahead Recipe #4, p. 260)

6 tablespoons low-fat milk

½ cup grated low-fat cheddar cheese

2 hot dogs, cut in half lengthwise, and chopped into small pieces

½ cup yellow cornmeal

½ cup Flour Blend (See Make-Ahead Recipe #8, p. 265)

2 teaspoons baking powder

¼ teaspoon salt

¼ teaspoon baking soda

Preheat oven to 375 degrees and line a muffin tin with paper liners. Spray liners lightly with cooking spray oil.

In a large mixing bowl, whisk together the eggs and sugar until well combined, then whisk in the melted butter, White Puree, milk, cheese, and hot dog pieces. In another mixing bowl, whisk together the cornmeal, Flour Blend, baking powder, salt, and baking soda. Fold the wet ingredients into the dry and mix until flour is just moistened (don't over-mix or the muffins will be dense).

Scoop the batter into muffin tins, filling just to the top. Bake for 22 to 24 minutes, until tops are golden brown and a toothpick inserted in the center comes out clean.

PER SERVING (1 MUFFIN, 71G): *Calories 138; Total Fat 5g; Fiber 1g; Total Carbohydrate 18g; Sugar 4g; Protein 7g; Sodium 288mg; Cholesterol 42mg; Calcium 110mg*

Make Mine a Mac 'n' Cheese Pizza

When you can combine three of your kid's top favorite foods (in this case, pizza, pasta ,and cheese) together with healthy ingredients, you know you have a winning recipe. The pizza sauce is already a healthy food because of its lycopene-laden tomatoes, and it also offers an ideal hiding spot for pureed white and orange vegetables. This is also the one way Missy gets some kids to eat whole-grain pasta because it's blanketed with the melted cheese, so they can't tell it's not their usual white noodles.

MAKES 8 SERVINGS

¾ cup store-bought pizza sauce

¼ cup **White or Orange Puree (See Make-Ahead Recipe #4, p. 260, or #2, p. 258)**

1 large (about 12-inch) store-bought pizza crust, ideally whole grain (like Boboli® whole grain)

1 cup *cooked* elbow pasta, ideally whole grain

1½ cups part-skim shredded mozzarella cheese

Preheat oven to 450 degrees and preheat a pizza stone, if using one, or spray a baking sheet with oil.

In a mixing bowl, combine pizza sauce with White or Orange Puree. Mix well. Spread sauce evenly over pizza crust. Scatter cooked pasta evenly over the sauce, then top with shredded cheese. Bake for 10 to 12 minutes until cheese is melted, bubbly, and golden brown.

Allow to cool a few minutes, then cut into wedges and serve.

PER SERVING (1 SLICE, 101G): *Calories 193; Total Fat 7g; Fiber 5g; Total Carbohydrate 24g; Sugar 2g; Protein 11g; Sodium 332mg; Cholesterol 18mg; Calcium 180mg*

Supercharged Tuna Sliders

These days, anything served on a soft, little bun can be called a "slider." Missy loves them because they're the "anti-supersize" lunch. That said, her version is supercharged with hidden whole grains and pureed white beans, which increase the protein and replace some of the fat found in traditional tuna salad.

MAKES 8 SLIDERS (4 SERVINGS)

2 tablespoons White Bean Puree (see Make-Ahead Recipe #7, p. 264)

2 to 3 tablespoons low-fat mayonnaise

2 tablespoons wheat germ

1 (6-ounce) can "chunk light" tuna, packed in water, drained

Salt, freshly ground pepper, and freshly squeezed lemon juice, to taste

8 small soft dinner rolls (ideally whole wheat)

½ cup low-fat shredded cheddar cheese

Pickle and/or small tomato slices, for garnish, optional

Preheat oven to 400 (?) degrees and line a baking sheet with parchment paper or foil.

In a mixing bowl, use a fork to combine the White Bean Puree, mayonnaise, wheat germ, and tuna. Season with salt, pepper, and lemon juice to taste. Cut dinner rolls horizontally in half and place all 16 halves on the baking sheet. Divide the tuna equally among the rolls, top with about one tablespoon of cheese and bake, open-faced, for 2 to 3 minutes until cheese is melted. Remove from oven, garnish with pickles and/or tomato, if using, close sandwiches, and serve.

> **PER SERVING (2 SLIDERS, 127G):** *Calories 260; Total Fat 7g; Fiber 5g; Total Carbohydrate 32g; Sugar 5g; Protein 20g; Sodium 548mg; Cholesterol 18mg; Calcium 130mg*

Hot Doggitos

Hot dog meets bean burrito—the Sneaky Chef way. Who would have guessed that a simple can of low-fat re-fried beans could help aid and abet hidden veggie puree? Not only that, but these healthy burritos are a perfect, portable fast food, especially when you wrap them in wax paper for that authentic drive-thru feel. Missy preps these up to one day in advance for good at-home or lunch box (if there's a microwave available) eating.

This recipe is not advised for kids under 3, as hot dogs can pose a choking hazard.

MAKES 4 SERVINGS

4 hot dogs, ideally without nitrates

½ cup canned low-fat refried beans

¼ **cup White Puree (See Make-Ahead Recipe #4, p. 260)**

2 tablespoons salsa

4 (10- to 12-inch) flour tortillas, ideally whole wheat

½ cup low-fat shredded cheddar cheese, divided

PER SERVING (1 DOGGITO, 191G):
Calories 466; Total Fat 23g; Fiber 4g; Total Carbohydrate 38g; Sugar 0g; Protein 18g; Sodium 784mg; Cholesterol 38mg; Calcium 110mg

Cook hot dogs according to package directions. Set aside.

In a mixing bowl, combine refried beans, White Puree, and salsa. Place tortillas between moist paper towels and microwave on high for 30 seconds to soften. Spoon 2 to 3 tablespoons of the bean mixture onto the bottom half of each tortilla. Top with the hot dog and 1 to 2 tablespoons of cheese. Fold the end of the tortilla closest to you over the filling ingredients and then tuck the right end in and roll up. One end of the burrito is left open and unfolded. Repeat with the remaining burritos.

Wrap in wax or parchment paper, and serve immediately, or refrigerate for up to 2 days. Simply reheat for 30 seconds in the microwave when you're ready to serve.

Crackle & Pop Peanut Butter Sandwich

Many kids dislike crunchy peanut butter, but you don't have to forgo giving PB a little crunchy zip. Rice Krispies™ give this simple sandwich a pop-in-your-mouth, surprising twist. Use it as you would sprinkles on ice cream to distract your kids from the whole grains and veggie puree hidden inside.

MAKES 1 SERVING

2 tablespoons creamy peanut butter

1 to 2 tablespoons Orange Puree (see Make-Ahead Recipe #2, p. 258)

1 tablespoon wheat germ

1 to 2 tablespoons crispy brown rice cereal (or Rice Krispies®)

Two slices bread, ideally whole grain

Jam or banana slices, optional

In a bowl, using the back of a fork, mix peanut butter with Orange Puree and wheat germ. Spread onto both sides of the bread, add jam or banana slices, if using, and crispy brown rice cereal. Close sandwich, slice, and serve.

PER SERVING (1 SANDWICH, 101G): *Calories 371; Total Fat 20g; Fiber 7g; Total Carbohydrate 35g; Sugar 5g; Protein 17g; Sodium 339mg; Cholesterol 0mg; Calcium 70mg*

DINNER

Clever Crepes—For Dinner

Just like the breakfast versions on page 175, dinner-time crepes are quick, tasty, and the perfect way to deliver some camouflaged nutrition. See the easy breakfast recipe for the crepe itself (or substitute a soft flour tortilla). The variations below are sure to add a little French flair to your family dinner.

MAKES 2 SERVINGS

BBQ Chicken Crepes:

2 tablespoons store-bought BBQ sauce

2 tablespoons White Puree
   (see Make-Ahead Recipe #4, p. 260)

2 clever crepes (p. 175) or soft tortillas

4 ounces chicken strips, cooked

2 slices low-fat Swiss or Gruyere cheese

In a mixing bowl, combine BBQ sauce and White Puree. Heat a small pan and lay crepe down; spread BBQ sauce mixture on crepe, top with chicken and cheese, and fold in half, then half again to make a square. Heat until cheese is melted. Repeat with second crepe.

> **PER SERVING (1 CREPE, 160G):** *Calories 300; Total Fat 8g; Fiber 3g; Total Carbohydrate 34g; Sugar 5g; Protein 23g; Sodium 794mg; Cholesterol 59mg; Calcium 380mg*

Ham and Cheese Crepes:

2 teaspoons honey mustard

2 tablespoons Orange Puree

  (see Make-Ahead Recipe #2, p. 258)

2 crepes (or soft tortillas)

2 slices ham

2 slices low-fat Swiss or Gruyere cheese

In a mixing bowl, combine honey mustard with Orange Puree. Heat a small pan and lay crepe down; spread mustard sauce mixture on crepe, top with a slice of ham and cheese, and fold in half, then half again to make a square. Heat until cheese is melted. Repeat with second crepe.

PER SERVING (1 CREPE, 129G): *Calories 261; Total Fat 7g; Fiber 3g; Total Carbohydrate 32g; Sugar 3g; Protein 18g; Sodium 748mg; Cholesterol 22mg; Calcium 380mg*

Q: My kids only eat white bread and white pasta. How can get some whole grains into them?

A: Recently, "whole wheat white" breads and pasta blends have been popping up on grocery store shelves, and they make a great starting place to gently acclimate children's palates to whole grain. As they get more accustomed to the hybrids, you can start introducing 100 percent whole-grain products to their plate. You can also create your own Sneaky Chef Flour Blend by mixing all-purpose flour with whole-grain flour and wheat germ, and use that in all your homemade baked goods as Missy does in her recipes.

Race Ya! Rice Balls

veggie whole grains anti oxidant boost protein boost low sugar

It's sometimes a challenge to get some kids to sit down to a bowl of steamed brown rice. Why fight it when you can disguise it? Convert rice into this hand-held side dish and finish it off in a hot oven to give the outside a nice crispness while keeping the inside cheesy and moist.

MAKES 8 SERVINGS

1 large egg

½ cup grated Parmesan cheese, divided

1 teaspoon dried oregano and/or basil

1 tablespoon tomato paste

2 tablespoons Orange or White Puree (see Make-Ahead Recipe #2 or #4, p. 258 or p. 260)

¼ cup wheat germ, divided

2 cups cooked brown rice, ideally short-grain

Marinara sauce, for serving, optional

Preheat oven to 450 degrees and generously spray a baking sheet with cooking spray.

Whisk together the egg, ¼ cup of the Parmesan cheese, the spices, tomato paste, Orange or White Puree, and 2 tablespoons of the oat bran or wheat germ. Add rice and mix well. Pour remaining parmesan and oat bran/wheat germ onto a plate and set aside.

Using damp hands, pinch off about 1 tablespoonful of the rice mixture and shape into small balls. Roll each ball in the oat bran or wheat germ and parmesan mixture, coating fully.

Gently place the rice balls on the prepared sheet, generously spray the tops of the balls with more cooking spray, and bake for

5 minutes. Using a spatula to loosen, turn the rice balls over, then return them to the oven for another 5 minutes to brown on the other side. Serve with salt and pepper. Serve as a handheld side dish or dipped in marinara sauce (with additional added White or Orange Puree, of course!).

PER SERVING (68G): *Calories 100; Total Fat 3g; Fiber 1g; Total Carbohydrate 14g; Sugar 0g; Protein 5g; Sodium 107mg; Cholesterol 32mg; Calcium 80mg*

Spaghetti Fit-Tatta

This is a full meal in one skillet, meaning less prep time and fewer dishes. You'll also have fewer leftovers, as kids will clean their plates, despite the protein and veggies inside.

MAKES 8 SERVINGS

½ cup store-bought tomato sauce

½ cup White Puree (see Make-Ahead Recipe #4, p. 260)

3 ounces deli turkey or cooked chicken, diced

2 cups cooked spaghetti, ideally whole-grain

2 large eggs

4 egg whites (or ¾ cup liquid egg whites)

¾ cup shredded low-fat cheddar or mozzarella cheese, divided

Salt and freshly ground black pepper, to taste

Optional extras: ½ cup each sliced: mushrooms, onions, cooked ham, or bacon

PER SERVING (112G): *Calories 121; Total Fat 3g; Fiber 2g; Total Carbohydrate 15g; Sugar 2g; Protein 11g; Sodium 133mg; Cholesterol 62mg; Calcium 70mg*

Preheat oven to 400 degrees.

In a large mixing bowl, combine the tomato sauce with White Puree, diced turkey or chicken, and any of the optional extras. Using tongs, toss the spaghetti with the sauce mixture. Heat an 8-inch or 10-inch oven-proof skillet over medium heat and spray bottom generously with cooking spray. Pour spaghetti mixture into the pan and spread evenly.

In the same mixing bowl, beat the eggs and egg whites with ¼ cup of the cheese and pour over spaghetti mixture. Let cook without stirring until almost fully set, about 10 minutes. Sprinkle the remaining cheese evenly over the top and place the skillet in oven until the cheese is melted and bubbly, about 10 minutes. Remove and slice into wedges to serve.

Teach Kids How to Eat Out

You won't always be there when your tweens are deciding what to eat. Give them some guidance before they're in line at the movies, in the cafeteria, or at a fast-food place with friends, so they know how to make a choice that's yummy—and healthy. Here are some tips to share:

- Choose popcorn with no added butter or salt at the movies.
- Instead of movie theater candy, enjoy a refreshing low-fat frozen yogurt or ice cream.
- Still want some candy? Choose dark chocolate-covered raisins or peanuts.
- If you must have soda, order just one and ask for extra "courtesy cups," then give everyone a small portion.
- Go for soup (especially lower-fat "red" or broth-based not creamy "white" soups), salad, or turkey sandwiches at the lunch cafeteria.
- Skip the school's vending machine and opt for fresh fruit or fruit salad and yogurt from the cafeteria instead.
- Take your cafeteria tray out of the line for "white" foods such as mashed potatoes, French fries, white bread, and potato chips, and instead head for the colorful foods such as fresh fruit and veggies.
- At your next fast food pit stop, make it a "single" hamburger, not a double, and hold the cheese and special (a.k.a. fattening) sauce. Add extra pickles and ketchup for extra flavor.
- Choose pre-cut "apple fries" instead of french fries if they're offered.
- Skip the soda and order water or low-fat milk with the meal.
- Hold the mayo on the sandwich and add extra non-fat ketchup or mustard instead.

"I'm a Vegetarian This Week" Burger

veggie · whole grains · anti oxidant boost · low sugar · protein boost

Fickle tweens frequently become overnight vegetarians, thanks to friends, movies, books, or other influences. But don't let the name fool you—this doesn't always mean they'll eat more veggies, and can end up meaning they'll eat more carbs and not enough protein. Missy calls them "carb-etarians!" Your tween's vegetarian lifestyle may not last forever, but in the meantime, this recipe offers complete protein in a meatless burger. Add a few pickle slices and ketchup, and even the carnivores in your house will like them!

MAKES 4 SERVINGS

¼ cup cooked brown rice

¼ cup rolled oats

¼ cup canned white beans, drained and rinsed

¼ cup grated parmesan cheese

1 cup raw cauliflower, chopped

1 cup raw mushrooms, chopped

½ teaspoon onion

½ teaspoon garlic powder

3 tablespoons ketchup, plus more for serving

6 tablespoons whole-wheat flour

Salt and freshly ground pepper, to taste

Hamburger buns

Pickles, for garnish, optional

Load all of the ingredients except the flour into a food processor and puree on high until completely smooth. Add flour and process just until mixed in.

Using lightly oiled hands, form 4 patties. Wrap and refrigerate or freeze until ready to cook, or cook immediately. Heat a griddle pan on medium high, spray well with cooking spray, and sear one side of the burger quickly, then spray the top with more oil and flip to sear the other side; reduce heat to medium-low and continue to cook through fully, about 5 to 7 more minutes. Season with salt and freshly ground pepper, to taste.

Serve on buns with pickles and ketchup, if desired.

PER SERVING (1 BURGER, 93G): *Calories 144; Total Fat 3g; Fiber 4g; Total Carbohydrate 23g; Sugar 1g; Protein 8g; Sodium 106mg; Cholesterol 6mg; Calcium 100mg*

Honey BBQ Chicken Nuggets

There's something about chicken nuggets that make them one of the most popular kid foods in America! Missy uses it to her sneaky advantage. She substitutes "oven-frying" for deep-frying, and upgrades the breading so it becomes a nutritious food instead of just a layer of simple carbs to hold the frying fat. The dipping sauce can also add delicious covert nutrition—especially when you add spinach and blueberries to it.

MAKES 4 SERVINGS

½ cup whole-wheat flour

2 large egg whites (about 6 tablespoons liquid egg whites)

½ cup Purple or Orange Puree (see Make-Ahead Recipe #1, p. 257 or #2, p. 258), divided

½ cup store-bought BBQ sauce, divided

2 tablespoons honey, divided

½ cup ground flax or wheat germ

1 cup crushed whole-grain cereal flakes (from about 2 cups of cereal)

1 pound boneless, skinless chicken breasts, cut into small nuggets

Salt and freshly ground pepper, to taste

Place flour in a shallow dish or on a plate. In another shallow bowl, beat egg whites with ¼ cup of the Purple or Orange Puree, ¼ cup of the BBQ sauce, and 1 tablespoon of the honey and place next to the flour. In a third shallow dish or on a paper plate, combine the ground flax and crushed cereal. Place remaining puree, BBQ sauce, and honey in a clean bowl and set aside to use as dipping sauce.

Dredge each piece of chicken in the flour, shaking off excess, then dip in the egg mixture, followed by the cereal mixture. Press the breading evenly onto both sides of the chicken. Put on wax or parchment paper and store in the refrigerator for cooking tomorrow or proceed to cook immediately.

Pan-fry method (higher fat and longer time standing at stove, but crispier):

Heat 2 tablespoons oil in a large skillet over moderately high heat until hot but not smoking. Add several nuggets of chicken at a time, pan-frying on one side until the crumbs look golden, about 2 to 3 minutes. Watch for burning, and turn down heat if necessary. With tongs, turn the pieces over and cook until golden, about 3 minutes. Reduce the heat to low until cooked through, about another 10 minutes. Blot cooked nuggets on paper towels to remove excess oil.

Oven-bake method (not as brown and crisp, but lower fat and less time standing at stove):

Preheat oven to 400 degrees.

Place breaded nuggets on a lightly sprayed cookie sheet and bake for 10 to 12 minutes. Turn chicken nuggets over once with tongs, then return to oven for another 10 to 12 minutes until cooked through.

Season with salt and freshly ground pepper, to taste. Serve with honey BBQ dipping sauce.

PER SERVING (144G): *Calories 323; Total Fat 8g; Fiber 9g; Total Carbohydrate 54g; Sugar 21g; Protein 13g; Sodium 224mg; Cholesterol 10mg; Calcium 730mg*

Sneaky Panini

Panini—warm, grilled, cheesy sandwiches—are all the rage now, but the ones made in restaurants can be more caloric than a slice of pizza. So Missy has improved this normally decadent dish with some whole grains, veggie purees, and lower fat cheese (although Missy dares not call this recipe diet food!). No fancy panini press needed—you can make this in a skillet or even your waffle iron! This is a dinner winner!

MAKES 4 SERVINGS

2 tablespoons whole-wheat flour

1 egg white (about 3 tablespoons liquid
   egg whites)

3 tablespoons White Puree
   (see Make-Ahead Recipe #4, p. 260)

2 tablespoons wheat germ

2 tablespoons ground flax

2 tablespoons grated Parmesan cheese

2 thin chicken cutlets (about ½ pound)

¼ cup tomato sauce

4 slices sourdough or other rustic Italian
   bread, ideally whole-grain

2 slices part-skim mozzarella (or provolone)
   cheese, divided

Salt and freshly ground pepper, to taste

Preheat the oven to 400 degrees. Spray a baking sheet with cooking spray.

Place the flour in a shallow dish or plate. In another shallow dish, beat the egg white together with 1½ tablespoons of the White Puree and set the mixture next to the flour. In a third shallow dish or on a paper plate, combine the wheat germ, flax, and Parmesan cheese.

Dredge each piece of chicken in the flour; shake off the excess. Then dip the chicken in the egg mixture, followed by the wheat germ mixture. Press the breading evenly onto both sides of the chicken.

Put the breaded chicken on parchment paper and store in the refrigerator for cooking tomorrow or proceed to cook immediately.

Place the breaded chicken on the prepared baking sheet. Spray the top of the chicken generously with oil and bake for 10 to 12 minutes. With a spatula, turn the cutlets over, spray them with oil, then bake for another 10 to 12 minutes, until chicken is cooked through.

Assemble and cook sandwiches:

In a mixing bowl, combine the tomato sauce with remaining White Puree. Lay slices of bread on a cutting board and spread about 1 tablespoon tomato sauce mixture on each slice of bread, then top with 1 tablespoon cheese. Top four of the slices with chicken and close sandwiches.

Heat a large (10- or 12-inch) nonstick skillet over moderately high heat and spray generously with cooking spray. Add one or two sandwiches at a time, spray the tops of the sandwiches with more oil, and cook until the bread is golden brown and the cheese is melted, flipping once. Press occasionally with a strong spatula. Remove from pan, slice sandwiches, and serve half to each person.

PER SERVING (½ SANDWICH, 89G): *Calories 198; Total Fat 7g; Fiber 4g; Total Carbohydrate 23g; Sugar 4g; Protein 12g; Sodium 245mg; Cholesterol 13mg; Calcium 180mg*

BBQ Pulled Pork Sandwiches

BBQ sauce is full of flavor and opportunities to hide Sneaky Chef fruit and vegetable purees! Plus, you can easily replicate the smoky, slow-simmered flavors of a Colorado ranch smokehouse in just a few minutes. Missy uses lower fat pork tenderloin in this braised recipe—even though traditional recipes call for higher fat cuts of pork, like shoulder. Low-fat pork pairs naturally with the tang of cherry, pomegranate, and tomato paste. Simmer on low heat on the stovetop or combine in a slow cooker, and this dish will be ready for a bun anytime your gang comes home for dinner.

MAKES 4 SERVINGS

1 pork tenderloin (1 to 1½ pounds)

1 cup vegetable or chicken broth

1 cup Cherry Puree* (see Make-Ahead Recipe #6, p. 263)

¼ cup apple cider vinegar

1 (6-ounce) can tomato paste

½ cup store-bought BBQ sauce

½ cup pomegranate juice

1 teaspoon chili powder

Salt, freshly ground black pepper, and hot sauce, to taste

4 hamburger buns or sandwich rolls, ideally whole-grain

*Alternatively, you can mix ½ cup Cherry Puree with ½ cup Orange Puree, see Make-Ahead Recipe #2, p. 258)

Combine all the ingredients except the tenderloin and buns in a large saucepan. Add the tenderloin and turn to coat. Bring to a boil over high heat, then reduce to a gentle simmer, cover, and cook for about an hour, stirring occasionally.

Remove pork from saucepan and shred using two forks. While shredding, raise heat and boil the sauce to thicken it slightly. Return shredded pork to the saucepan and toss with the sauce. Season with salt, freshly ground pepper, and/or hot sauce, to taste. Serve on lightly-toasted hamburger buns.

PER SERVING (1 SANDWICH, 426G): *Calories 404; Total Fat 5g; Fiber 7g; Total Carbohydrate 61g; Sugar 33g; Protein 31g; Sodium 589mg; Cholesterol 54mg; Calcium 80mg*

Off the Couch Potato Skins

healthy fats   protein boost   anti oxidant boost   low sugar

*"No Sin Potato Skins" were one of the most popular recipes in Missy's first book, **The Sneaky Chef.** Adding chicken gives it more protein and transforms a fun appetizer into a complete meal. Missy especially loves that there are almost no dishes to wash—Hooray!*

MAKES 4 SERVINGS

2 large russet potatoes, scrubbed

2 tablespoons extra-virgin olive oil, divided

½ teaspoon coarse kosher salt

¼ **cup White Puree (see Make Ahead Recipe #4, p. 260)**

½ cup low-fat shredded cheddar or Colby cheese, divided

½ cup cooked chicken, diced , divided

2 tablespoons bacon bits, optional, divided

Optional dip: Greek-style plain yogurt or low-fat sour cream

Preheat oven to 450 degrees and spray a baking sheet with cooking spray.

Prick potatoes several times with a fork and place them on the baking sheet. Rub skins with one tablespoon of the olive oil, sprinkle lightly with coarse salt, and bake for 50 to 60 minutes until tender. Remove potatoes from the oven and set aside until cool enough to handle.

Cut potatoes in half lengthwise and carefully scoop out the flesh, leaving about ¼-inch-thick shells.

Place shells, skin side down, on the prepared baking sheet and brush the insides with the remaining olive oil. With the back of a spoon, spread about one tablespoon of White

Puree on the inside of each potato skin, covering the surface evenly. Top with about 2 tablespoons of diced chicken, a sprinkling of bacon bits (if using), and top off with 2 tablespoons of cheese per skin.

Return to oven for 5 to 7 minutes until bubbly brown. Serve with a dollop of Greek-style plain yogurt or low-fat sour cream, if desired.

PER SERVING (241G): *Calories 268; Total Fat 10g; Fiber 3g; Total Carbohydrate 34g; Sugar 2g; Protein 12g; Sodium 401mg; Cholesterol 17mg; Calcium 90mg*

Sammy's Sweet 'n' Sour Salad (SSSS)

*One afternoon, Missy enlisted her girls and their friends' support in a brainstorming session for recipe ideas. What better way to find out what kids **really** crave! After coming up with a bunch of ideas (many of which ended up in this book), they all got up and ran to the kitchen to start cooking up their own concoctions. Missy's younger daughter, Sammy, created this deliciously crunchy salad and tossed it all with a sweet and sour dressing. She even wrote up all the ingredients and instructions herself and stuck the paper to the refrigerator door. It's become a family fave and just highlights that it's amazing what kids will eat if they make it themselves!*

MAKES 4 SERVINGS

1 (15-ounce) can chickpeas, rinsed

4 cups romaine lettuce, chopped small

1 sweet bell pepper, chopped small

2 tablespoons slivered almonds

2 tablespoons grated parmesan cheese

Salt and freshly ground black pepper, to taste

2 teaspoons apple cider vinegar

2 tablespoons low-fat Ranch dressing
   or French dressing

Toss all ingredients except vinegar and dressing in a mixing bowl. Add vinegar and dressing and toss to coat salad evenly.

PER SERVING (233G): *Calories 193; Total Fat 7g; Fiber 10g; Total Carbohydrate 33g; Sugar 7g; Protein 12g; Sodium 89mg; Cholesterol 3mg; Calcium 110mg*

SNACKS, TREATS & DRINKS

Easy, Cheesy Chips

Missy rarely allows her girls to eat Doritos®, so her daughter Emily had the idea for homemade ones. Missy's version, made with corn tortilla chips, is fun and easy—it takes less that 30 minutes from start to finish. Kids love to brush the tortillas with oil and cut them with scissors. Plus, they're an inexpensive and healthier alternative to bags of deep-fried chips.

MAKES 8 DOZEN CHIPS (ABOUT 8 SERVINGS)

½ teaspoon salt

½ teaspoon onion powder

½ teaspoon garlic powder

½ teaspoon paprika

3 tablespoons ground flax seeds

½ cup grated Romano cheese

12 (6-inch) corn tortillas

2 tablespoons extra-virgin olive oil

Preheat oven to 400 degrees.

Combine the salt, onion powder, garlic powder, paprika, and flax in a bowl. Pour oil into another small bowl. Using a pastry brush, brush both sides of each tortilla with oil. Stack 6 of them together and use kitchen shears or scissors to cut the stack into 8 triangles, for a total of 48 chips. Repeat with the remaining 6 tortillas. Scatter the chips in a single layer onto one or two large baking sheets and sprinkle them evenly with the spice mixture and Romano cheese. Bake 12 to 14 minutes, flipping once and checking occasionally so they don't burn, until crispy and golden brown.

Serve with Intro to Hummus (p. 202) or Cheese Fun-Do.

PER SERVING (8 CHIPS, 36G): *Calories 111; Total Fat 5g; Fiber 2g; Total Carbohydrate 13g; Sugar 0g; Protein 4g; Sodium 168mg; Cholesterol 6mg; Calcium 110mg*

Cheese Fun-Do

One snowy Sunday, two of Emily's "BFFs," Paige and Rebecca, were over rehearsing at Missy's house for the fifth grade talent show. Missy grabbed them from the "stage" to help taste test various versions of this cheese fondue. Rebecca, who in the past had declared she wouldn't eat fruit—no way, no how— needed no prompting to skewer a fresh, crisp apple before dipping into the fondue. Paige said, "I wish my mom would make this for me after school every day!" When they ran out of apples, Missy slipped some broccoli onto the skewers, and they used it to scoop up every last drop of cheesy gooiness. When the bowl was picked clean, they bounced back to the stage, re-energized and ready to rock.

MAKES 1 CUP (ABOUT 4 SERVINGS)

6 ounces Swiss, Gruyere, or American cheese,
    ideally low-fat

2 teaspoons cornstarch

½ cup apple cider or apple juice

1½ teaspoons apple cider vinegar

½ teaspoon honey mustard

**¼ cup White Puree (see Make-Ahead
    Recipe #4, p. 260)**

Whole-grain or sourdough bread cubes,
    broccoli, cauliflower, chunks of ham
    and/or apple, for dipping

In a mixing bowl, toss the grated cheese with the cornstarch. In a saucepan, heat the apple cider, vinegar, honey mustard, and White Puree over medium heat until it just starts to boil.* Immediately reduce heat to medium-low and stir in the cheese mixture, one handful at a time. Let each addition of cheese melt before adding more. Stir frequently. Serve hot with dipping items on skewers. This sauce thickens as it cools, so if there is a delay in serving it, simply put it back in the microwave for another 15 to 30 seconds.

*Quicker microwave method: Mix all ingredients in a microwave-safe bowl. Cover the bowl with a wet paper towel and microwave on high for 30 seconds at a time until fully melted.

PER SERVING (84G): *Calories 97; Total Fat 2g; Fiber 0g; Total Carbohydrate 7g; Sugar 4g; Protein 12g; Sodium 115mg; Cholesterol 15mg; Calcium 410mg*

Quick Tip!

Out of sight, out of mind: If your kids don't see sugary snacks, they'll be less likely to hound you for them. Fill up your cookie jars with granola, whole-wheat crackers, or dried fruit. Display colorful fruits in a bowl that kids can reach, and store low-fat cheeses, yogurts, and cut-up veggies at your kids' eye level in the fridge.

Rock 'n' Roll-Up Pizza Sticks

Missy has fallen in love with ready-made pizza dough and all the fun, simple, things you can make with it! Cheese sticks are the perfect shape for rolling up in dough, and they melt very well inside. The puree disappears into the cheesy gooeyness, so no one will be the wiser.

MAKES 4 SERVINGS

4 teaspoons tomato paste

4 teaspoons Orange Puree (see Make-Ahead Recipe #2, p. 258)

2 teaspoons ground flax seeds

8 ounces store-bought pizza dough, ideally whole-grain

4 part-skim mozzarella cheese sticks

Diced ham or other meat, optional

Preheat oven to 400 degrees.

In a mixing bowl, combine tomato paste, Orange Puree, and flax. Working on a clean cutting board, pinch off about two ounces of pizza dough and stretch (or roll) it into a rectangle shape. Spread about 2 teaspoons of the tomato mixture on each piece of dough, lay a cheese stick in middle of dough, top with diced ham, if using, and roll up, pinching the ends to seal and completely cover the cheese stick.

Refrigerate or freeze for later use, or proceed to bake immediately for 15 to 20 minutes until the dough is golden brown.

PER SERVING (SERVING SIZE 1 STICK, 93G): *Calories 226; Total Fat 8g; Fiber 4g; Total Carbohydrate 32g; Sugar 1g; Protein 12g; Sodium 391mg; Cholesterol 15mg; Calcium 210mg*

Sneaky S'mores

S'mores are a gooey, yummy, all-American camping and cook-out tradition, but they're usually a once-in-a-while indulgence. With Missy's guiltless version, however, this sweet treat can be in your kids' regular rotation. They'll never tire of the classic combo of marshmallow and chocolate chips, and you'll never spill that there's a healthy, whole-grain cookie underneath!

MAKES 2 DOZEN

1½ cup Flour Blend (*see Make-Ahead Recipe #8, p. 265*)

½ teaspoon baking soda

½ teaspoon salt

½ teaspoon cinnamon

6 tablespoons unsalted butter, softened

½ cup light brown sugar, packed

1 large egg yolk

½ cup Orange Puree (*see Make-Ahead Recipe #2, p. 258*)

1 teaspoon pure vanilla extract

1 cup semi-sweet chocolate chips, divided

1 cup mini marshmallows

Preheat oven to 350 degrees.

In a large bowl, whisk together Flour Blend, baking soda, salt, and cinnamon. Set aside.

In the bowl of an electric mixer, beat the butter and sugar until creamy. Beat in egg yolk, Orange Puree, and vanilla. Add dry ingredients and mix on low speed. Stir in ½ cup of the chocolate chips. Pinch off tablespoon amounts of dough and roll about 24 balls in your hands (wet your hands with water or spray them with oil to keep from sticking to dough). Place on a parchment-lined cookie sheet about an inch apart. Gently press your thumb into the center of each ball to make a deep indent.

Bake 16 to 18 minutes, or until golden brown. Remove cookies from oven and fill each indent with a couple of chocolate chips and mini marshmallows. Return cookies to oven for 1 more minute to just slightly melt the marshmallows and chocolate chips.

PER SERVING (1 SMORE, 58G): *Calories 130; Total Fat 6g; Fiber 2g; Total Carbohydrate 19g; Sugar 12g; Protein 1g; Sodium 101mg; Cholesterol 12mg; Calcium 20mg*

Black Forest Cupcakes

Bring back the cupcake! Missy's always sad to hear that cupcakes are banned from schools and birthday parties. After all, not all cupcakes are equal, and not every cupcake deserves to be labeled as unhealthy. Some of these little treats can actually be pretty good for your kids. Take Missy's Black Forest version, for example. It has two of the world's healthiest fruits and wheat germ mixed right in. Bring them to your next bake sale, and there'll be no protest from kids—or their moms.

MAKES 18–24 CUPCAKES

3 large eggs

¾ cup Cherry Puree (see Make-Ahead Recipe #6, p. 263)

1 cup pure pomegranate (or cranberry) juice

½ teaspoon almond extract

¼ cup wheat germ

1 box (about 18 ounces) chocolate cake mix (such as Duncan Hines® Moist Deluxe® Devil's Food)

Vanilla frosting, grated chocolate (or chocolate chips) and/or whole cherries with stems, optional

Preheat oven to 350 degrees and line a muffin tin with paper muffin cups.

In the bowl of an electric mixer, combine all ingredients, except toppings. Blend at low speed for 30 seconds, then increase to medium speed for another 2 minutes. Pour batter into muffin tins. Bake for 19 to 21 minutes (until a toothpick inserted in the center comes out clean). Remove and cool before frosting, if desired. Use vanilla frosting with a little grated chocolate—or a few chocolate chips—and a whole cherry with stem on top.

PER SERVING (1 CUPCAKE, 43G): *Calories 115; Total Fat 4g; Fiber 1g; Total Carbohydrate 19g; Sugar 10g; Protein 2g; Sodium 190mg; Cholesterol 26mg; Calcium 40mg*

Sweet Strawberry Cupcakes

This recipe is a terrific way to turn the ordinary into the extraordinary! All you need is a box of yellow cake mix. The Strawberry Puree and cranberry juice will add a super boost of fiber, vitamin C, and antioxidants and will make the cupcakes even more moist and flavorful. Plus, none of your little shortcakes will ever guess there's heart-healthy oat bran stashed under those pretty pink sprinkles.

MAKES 18 ? CUPCAKES

3 large eggs

¾ cup Strawberry Puree (see Make-Ahead Recipe #5, p. 262)

1 cup cranberry juice

½ cup oat bran

1 box (about 18 ounces) yellow cake mix (such as Duncan Hines® Moist Deluxe® Classic Yellow Cake Mix) or strawberry cake mix (such as Duncan Hines® Moist Deluxe Strawberry Supreme®)

Pink sprinkles and pink vanilla frosting, optional

Preheat oven to 350 degrees and line a muffin tin with pink paper muffin cups.

In the bowl of an electric mixer, place all ingredients, except sprinkles, if using. Blend at low speed for 30 seconds, then increase to medium speed for another 2 minutes. Using a spoon, mix 2 tablespoons of pink sprinkles into the batter. Pour batter into muffin tins. Bake for 19 to 21 minutes (until a toothpick inserted in the center comes out clean). Remove and cool before frosting with strawberry or vanilla frosting with pink sprinkles.

PER SERVING (1 CUPCAKE, 51G): *Calories 109; Total Fat 3g; Fiber 1g; Total Carbohydrate 21g; Sugar 11g; Protein 2g; Sodium 150mg; Cholesterol 26mg; Calcium 40mg*

Crunchy Chocolate Clusters

Similar to the Go-Go Granola recipe, this chocolate version is a perfect sweet addition to your kid's lunchbox. The indulgent flavors of chocolate, butter, and brown sugar will keep the fact that there are also some of the most substantial nutrients on earth mixed in under wraps. With lots of fiber and protein, your kids will have energy that lasts all afternoon.

Note: The mini-muffin cups will give the clusters a uniform size and shape, but you can also press the mixture into a pan to make the clusters into bars.

MAKES ABOUT 2 DOZEN

½ cup Ground Walnuts (see Make-Ahead Recipe #10, p. 267)

1 cup rolled oats

2 tablespoons oat bran

2 tablespoons ground flax seeds

¼ teaspoon salt

½ cup semi-sweet chocolate chips

2 tablespoons unsalted butter

2 tablespoons brown sugar, packed

Toast Ground Walnuts and oats in a large 10- to 12-inch dry skillet over medium-low heat, stirring occasionally until lightly browned, about 5 minutes (reduce heat if starting to burn). Meanwhile, mix the chocolate chips, oat bran, flax, and salt in a large mixing bowl. Add the warm, toasted walnuts and oats to the mixing bowl and stir to combine. Wipe skillet with a paper towel, return it to the stovetop, and reduce heat to low. Add the butter and brown sugar, stirring until melted and foaming, about 1 minute. Pour the hot mixture into the mixing bowl and quickly toss to coat all ingredients.

Spoon about one tablespoon of the hot mixture into 24 mini muffin liners and press down with fingers. Refrigerate for up to a week, or freeze for up to 3 months.

PER SERVING (1 CLUSTER, 14G): *Calories 72; Total Fat 4g; Fiber 1g; Total Carbohydrate 7g; Sugar 4g; Protein 2g; Sodium 25mg; Cholesterol 1mg; Calcium 10mg*

10 Healthy Snacks to Pack for the Playground

■ Edamame (soybeans in the pod), boiled, lightly salted, and served cold

■ Low-fat string cheese

■ Snap peas, raw

■ Chickpeas, lightly roasted and sprinkled with a little sugar

■ Whole-grain crackers, with or without peanut butter, light cream cheese, or jam

■ Brown rice cakes, with or without peanut butter and jam

■ Yogurt tubes, frozen so they'll soften to the consistency of ice cream while they play

■ Sweet bell pepper, cut into strips

■ Whole-grain tortilla chips, homemade or store bought

■ Pistachios, in their shell (for kids over four years old)

Gold-Medal Graham Crackers with Chocolate Cream Dip

This creamy chocolate dip is loaded with calcium and protein and makes a delicious "mini-meal" when combined with whole-grain crackers or fruit.

MAKES 1 CUP (4 SERVINGS)

½ cup part-skim ricotta cheese

4 tablespoons low-fat cream cheese

¼ tablespoons Cherry Puree
  (see Make-Ahead Recipe #6, p. 263)

3 tablespoons chocolate syrup

Graham crackers, strawberries, apple chunks,
  or sliced bananas on skewers or
  toothpicks, for dipping

Place all of the ingredients (except the dippers) in a blender or the bowl of a processor and puree on high until smooth. Serve with dippers of choice!

PER SERVING (¼ CUP DIP, 49G): *Calories 90; Total Fat 3g; Fiber 1g; Total Carbohydrate 13g; Sugar 9g; Protein 3g; Sodium 83mg; Cholesterol 11mg; Calcium 60mg*

Chocolate-Chip Cheesecake Muffins

Statistics show that 90 percent of school-aged girls and 75 percent of boys are not getting enough calcium in their diets. Good luck getting them to drink more milk. Missy's sneaky solution? Give them the bone-building nutrient in a delicious way. Best yet, these calcium-rich muffins can be whipped up entirely in the blender or food processor, meaning more calcium for kids, less work for mom.

MAKES 12 MUFFINS

12 small round cookies, like Nilla Wafers®
 or ¾ cup Graham Crust (recipe follows)

8 ounces light cream cheese, at room
 temperature

1 large egg

2 egg whites

⅔ cup **White Bean Puree**
 (see **Make-Ahead #7, p. 264**)

1 cup part-skim ricotta cheese

1 tablespoon pure vanilla extract

¾ cup sugar

½ teaspoon salt

2 tablespoons all-purpose flour

2 tablespoons semi-sweet chocolate chips,
 ideally "mini"

Preheat oven to 350 degrees, line a muffin tin with paper muffin cups, and drop a cookie onto the bottom of each cup (flat side up). Alternatively, press 1 tablespoon of Graham Crust into the bottom of each muffin cup.

Place all of the remaining ingredients (except the crust or cookies or chocolate chips) in a blender or the bowl of a food processor and puree on high until very smooth. Fill each prepared muffin cup with about ¼ cup of filling, drop in a few chocolate chips into each, and bake for 37 to 40 minutes, until the center of each muffin is set and edges are lightly browned. Chill for at least 30 minutes before serving.

Graham Crust:

MAKES 1 CRUST OR 1 CUP

½ cup chocolate or cinnamon graham
    crackers, crushed (measure before
    crushing)

¼ cup ground flax

¼ cup wheat germ

½ teaspoon cinnamon

3 tablespoons butter, melted

Mix all ingredients in a bowl. Use as directed.

Quick Tip!

In the mood for ice cream? Make it with an old fashioned ice-cream machine. Your kids will have to crank and churn it before they can indulge. Try it with Sneaky Chef Breakfast Ice Cream: Mix together and churn ½ cups pureed frozen strawberries, ½ cup milk, and 2 tablespoons honey or sugar.

PER SERVING (SERVING SIZE 1 MUFFIN, 96G):
Calories 183; Total Fat 6g; Fiber 1g; Total Carbohydrate 25g; Sugar 16g; Protein 7g; Sodium 239mg; Cholesterol 36mg; Calcium 90mg

Blue-Ribbon Ice Cream Sandwich

Although Missy's put this recipe in the dessert section, its blueberries, milk, and ricotta cheese have such a high nutrition content that it can also be a wholesome mini-meal snack. No ice cream maker necessary—you can make this in your mini food processor in 2 minutes flat.

MAKES 2 DOZEN SANDWICHES

¾ cup fresh or frozen
blueberries, no syrup
or sugar added

½ cup part-skim ricotta

¼ cup low-fat milk

2 tablespoons sugar

48 vanilla wafers
(small cookies)

¼ tablespoons rainbow
sprinkles or mini
chocolate chips, optional

Place blueberries, ricotta, milk, and sugar in the bowl of a food processor and puree on high until very smooth. Freeze for at least an hour, then spoon about 1 tablespoon onto a vanilla cookie. Top with a second cookie to make a sandwich. If using, pour sprinkles or chocolate chips onto a plate and roll the sandwich in them to coat sides evenly. Individually wrap each sandwich (or place in small plastic bags) and freeze.

PER SERVING (1 SANDWICH, 19G): *Calories 41; Total Fat 1g; Fiber 0g; Total Carbohydrate 6g; Sugar 4g; Protein 1g; Sodium 26mg; Cholesterol 6mg; Calcium 20mg*

Purple Power Pops

When was the last time your kids licked spinach off a popsicle stick—and loved every slurp?! The sneaky Purple Puree of blueberries and spinach combined with grape juice makes for a sweet, refreshing, and antioxidant-rich treat. When it comes to superfoods, purple is the color to beat.

MAKES ABOUT 6 POPS

¾ cup red grape juice

¾ cup Purple Puree
(see Make-Ahead
Recipe #1, p. 257)

In a mixing bowl or pitcher, combine grape juice and Purple Puree. Pour into popsicle molds, insert stick, and freeze for at least 3 hours.

> **PER SERVING (1 POP, 52G):** *Calories 28; Total Fat 0g; Fiber 1g; Total Carbohydrate 7g; Sugar 6g; Protein 0g; Sodium 8mg; Cholesterol 11mg; Calcium 10mg*

Can't Be Beat Banana Ice Cream Pops

Bananas and yogurt—healthy, no? Never fear—the chocolate chips will hinder even the most skeptical kids from realizing they're eating a serving of fruit and calcium. Missy will confess this, however: She eats one every night herself when she starts craving a rich, but low-fat, low-calorie treat. They're even great for quick, on-the-go breakfasts. (Really!)

MAKES ABOUT 6 POPS

½ cup low-fat milk

½ cup vanilla (or banana) yogurt

2 large bananas

2 tablespoons sugar

¼ cup semi-sweet chocolate chips, ideally "mini", optional

Blend all ingredients except chocolate chips in a blender until smooth. Pour equal amounts in popsicle molds, then drop about one tablespoon of chocolate chips into each pop, if desired. Insert stick, and freeze for at least 3 hours.

PER SERVING (1 POP, 90G): *Calories 82; Total Fat 1g; Fiber 1g; Total Carbohydrate 18g; Sugar 13g; Protein 2g; Sodium 23mg; Cholesterol 2mg; Calcium 60mg*

Sneaker-Doodle Cookies

"Sneaker-doodles" are just like the ever-popular sugar cookies, Snickerdoodles, except Missy's have healthy wheat germ and white beans inside. You don't have to chill the dough, so you can whip up a batch quickly, too.

MAKES 2 DOZEN COOKIES

1 egg white

4 tablespoons butter, softened

¾ cup sugar

⅓ cup White Bean Puree (see Make-Ahead
   Recipe #7, p. 264)

1 teaspoon pure vanilla extract

1 cup Flour Blend (see Make-Ahead
   Recipe #8, p. 265)

½ teaspoon salt

For garnish: 1 teaspoon cinnamon and
   1 tablespoon sugar

Preheat oven to 350 degrees and spray a baking sheet with cooking spray (or line with parchment paper).

In a large mixing bowl, whisk together the egg white, softened butter, sugar, White Bean Puree, and vanilla.

In another large bowl, whisk together the Flour Blend and salt. Add the dry ingredients to the wet and mix well to form a soft batter. Drop tablespoonfuls of batter onto the baking sheets (Missy uses a melon baller sprayed with oil to dole out the dough), leaving about 1 inch between each cookie. Pour the remaining tablespoon of sugar and cinnamon onto a plate and set aside.

Spray the bottom of a juice glass (about 3 inches across) with cooking spray and dip glass bottom in the cinnamon-sugar mixture. Press tops of cookies lightly with the glass, flattening each cookie to about ½-inch thick. Mist the bottom of the glass with cooking spray and dip into cinnamon-sugar for each cookie. Bake cookies, about 12 to 15 minutes, until lightly browned around the edges.

PER SERVING (SERVING SIZE 1 COOKIE, 16G):
Calories 59; Total Fat 1g; Fiber 1g; Total Carbohydrate 12g; Sugar 7g; Protein 1g; Sodium 52mg; Cholesterol 1mg; Calcium 0mg

Quick Tip!

Make sure your little ones are well hydrated. It'll keep them energized, motivated, and energetic. Plus, some hunger pains aren't hunger pains at all, but your body telling you it is thirsty. Have lots of cold water on hand—colorful straws and cups will encourage kids to take a sip. And if you do serve juice, cut it with water, which will reduce the sugar content. Your kids will never know the difference.

Surprise-icle

Remember those childhood creamsicles on a hot summer day? Missy's version has the same classic orange and vanilla flavoring along with the daring addition of sweet orange veggie puree. The kids don't stop to think twice as they lick their sticky fingers.

MAKES ABOUT 6 POPS

½ cup orange juice
   (no pulp)
¼ cup **Orange Puree**
   (see Make-Ahead
   Recipe #2, p. 258)
½ cup vanilla yogurt
2 tablespoons sugar
Rainbow sprinkles,
   optional

Blend all ingredients except sprinkles together in a blender until smooth. Drop a few sprinkles (if desired) into each popsicle mold and then pour equal amounts of the mixture in each. Insert stick, and freeze for at least 3 hours.

PER SERVING (1 POP, 46G): *Calories 30; Total Fat 0g; Fiber 1g; Total Carbohydrate 6g; Sugar 17g; Protein 1g; Sodium 17mg; Cholesterol 1mg; Calcium 40mg*

Sneaky Snack Swaps

If your kids are like ours, they come home from school ravenous. But before you hand them a snack that may be filled with sugar and fat, giving them a fast energy boost but setting them up for hunger and crankiness a short time later, try one of these sneaky swaps.

CHOOSE THIS	INSTEAD OF THIS
Frozen yogurt, sorbet or sherbert	Ice cream
Baked potato chips	Fried potato chips
Real fruit leather	Gummy fruit snacks
Light (94 percent fat-free) popcorn	Full-fat popcorn
Frozen fruit popsicles	Ice cream pops
100 percent juice (diluted with water)	Fruit "drinks"
Fruit smoothies	Milkshakes
English muffins (ideally whole grain)	Bagels
Pretzels (ideally whole grain)	Spiced and fried chips
Dark or semi-sweet chocolate	Milk chocolate

Chocolate No-Ache Shake

Studies show that chocolate milk actually helps an athlete's muscle recovery even more effectively than traditional sports drinks! But why settle for traditional chocolate milk when you can secretly enhance the nutrition—and the taste—with antioxidant-packed cherries and potassium-rich bananas? Your little athletes will be flexing their muscles while they wipe off their chocolate moustaches.

MAKES 2 SERVINGS

¾ cup low-fat milk

1 large frozen banana

2 to 3 tablespoons
chocolate syrup

¼ cup Cherry Puree
(see Make-Ahead
Recipe #6, p. 263)

A few ice cubes

In the container of a blender, combine all ingredients and blend until smooth. Serve in a tall glass with a straw.

PER SERVING (1 SHAKE, 196G): *Calories 170; Total Fat 2g; Fiber 3g; Total Carbohydrate 36g; Sugar 20g; Protein 5g; Sodium 68mg; Cholesterol 4mg; Calcium 140mg*

No-Joe Latte

Kids love nothing better than having what the grownups have. This coffee-free latte may not give them the same jolt yours does, but it will give them a hefty dose of calcium and vitamin D, a nutrient most kids these days are lacking. This is one of the only ways Missy gets Emily, her tween, to drink milk anymore. Serve it in the evening, and the tryptophan will promote good sleep and the calcium and vitamin D will help growing bones during the nighttime "spurt" hours. Strong, healthy bones mean that they'll be grown up sooner than you think!

MAKES 2 SERVINGS

2 cups cold skim milk

1 to 2 tablespoons sugar

Dash pure vanilla extract
   (or vanilla powder)

Raw sugar, cinnamon sugar,
   or cocoa for garnish,
   optional

Pour cold milk, sugar, and vanilla into a bowl and whisk vigorously until foamy. Alternatively, place ingredients in a blender and blend on high for about 30 seconds. Pour into microwave-safe mugs and microwave on high for about one minute or until desired warmth. Dust with garnish, if using, and serve.

PER SERVING (1 LATTE, 251G): *Calories 109; Total Fat 0g; Fiber 0g; Total Carbohydrate 18g; Sugar 18g; Protein 8g; Sodium 127mg; Cholesterol 5mg; Calcium 300mg*

Sparkling Strawberry Float

You won't have a problem helping your kids meet their goal of 5 fruits and veggies a day with this fizzy fruit drink! Serve it at your child's next birthday party in champagne glasses (plastic ones, that is).

MAKES 4 TO 6 SERVINGS

1½ cups frozen strawberries (no sugar or syrup added)

1½ cups cranberry juice, divided

2 tablespoons sugar

1 teaspoon fresh squeezed lemon juice

4 cups sparkling water, divided

Four whole fresh strawberries, straws, and/or drink umbrellas, for garnish, optional

Place frozen strawberries, ½ cup of the cranberry juice, sugar, and lemon juice in the bowl of a food processor, cover, and process on high, stopping occasionally to scrape the contents to the bottom to make a smooth sorbet. Note: At this point, the sorbet will be very soft—if you prefer a firmer "scoop," simply pour sorbet into a plastic tub or glass baking dish, cover, and place in the freezer for at least an hour. When ready to serve, pour 1 cup of sparkling water and ¼ cup cranberry juice into each glass. Scoop about ¼ cup of sorbet into each glass. If desired, garnish each glass with a fresh strawberry, slightly split and placed on the rim of the glass, and serve with a straw and/or drink umbrella.

PER SERVING (1 FLOAT, 185G): *Calories 96; Total Fat 0g; Fiber 2g; Total Carbohydrate 25g; Sugar 21g; Protein 1g; Sodium 4mg; Cholesterol 0mg; Calcium 20mg*

Super Sports Cubes

Professional athletes may tout the benefits of commercially prepared sports drinks, but they don't tell you about the high prices and heaps of sugar that come in each gulp. Sneaky moms know that freezing the sports "aid" into icy cubes will give the glass an added fun factor. Made from frozen juice concentrate, they'll provide the perfect amount of sweetness as they melt into a glass of water. More importantly, these cubes are packed with antioxidants, which help with muscle recovery after exercise, so your amateur athlete will be ready to get back in the game fast.

MAKES 10 CUBES (ABOUT 1 OUNCE EACH)

¼ cup pomegranate, cranberry, or
   grape juice*

1 cup frozen lemonade (or orange juice)
   concentrate

⅛ teaspoon salt

*Note: If you prefer to make homemade fruit juice, simply add ½ cup water to Strawberry or Cherry Puree (see Make-Ahead Recipe #5, p. 262 or #6, p. 263), and pour through a fine-mesh strainer to remove the pulp.

Combine juice, frozen lemonade, and salt in a pitcher or glass bowl. Pour into standard ice cube trays, cover, and freeze until solid. Use one or two cubes per glass of cold water and serve.

PER SERVING (1 CUBE, 34G): *Calories 49, Total Fat 0g; Fiber 0g; Total Carbohydrate 12g; Sugar 11g; Protein 1g; Sodium 30mg; Cholesterol 0mg; Calcium 10mg*

Cold Buster

This sweet, frozen-fruit smoothie has a big dose of immune-boosting vitamin C and antioxidants, which may help ward off colds and flu. The surprise ingredient here, black tea, has been shown to build up germ-fighting powers. The honey not only sweetens the deal, but soothes sore throats and coughs, too.

MAKES 4 SERVINGS

2 cups brewed
   decaffeinated black
   tea, cooled

1 large orange, peeled

1 cup fresh or frozen
   strawberries, rinsed
   (If using frozen, use a
   brand without syrup
   or added sugar)

Juice from 1 fresh lemon

4 tablespoons honey

2 to 3 cups ice

Put all the ingredients in a blender and blend on high until smooth. Serve in a tall glass with a straw.

PER SERVING (225G): *Calories 98; Total Fat 0g; Fiber 2g; Total Carbohydrate 26g; Sugar 22g; Protein 1g; Sodium 5mg; Cholesterol 0mg; Calcium 30mg*

CHAPTER SEVEN:

Sneaky Chef's Original Make-Ahead Recipes

The recipes that follow are the secret weapons in Missy's healthy-eating arsenal. These purees and blends are made of superfoods—fruits, veggies, grains, beans, and nuts that are packed with essential nutrients, which our kids don't always get enough of. These recipes transform those good-for-you foods into a concentrated, easily hide-able and disguise-able form, so you can slip them into the meals and treats your kids love to eat—without them even realizing they are there. You don't need special ops-training to make the most of them, you just need a little time to prep and a willingness to engage in a healthy, covert operation.

You can even use these Make-Aheads in packaged and prepared foods to give them an unnoticeable nutrition boost. Spike the canned spaghetti sauce with a helping of Orange Puree, or whisk some White Bean Puree into your boxed pancake mix. You won't have to spend hours in the kitchen to give your kids hours of extra energy. Plus, some purees are made for you in the super-market, like applesauce, tomato paste, and baby food (carrots, sweet potatoes, blueber-ries, and green veggies work as instant substitutes for some of Missy's Make-Ahead purees).

Each of these Make-Aheads takes less than 10 minutes to whip up. Carve out a few minutes each week to make the ones you aim to use later. Pull out your handy food processor (Missy uses a mini-processor be-cause they're easy to store and inexpensive) or a blender, but keep in mind you may have to add a bit more liquid than the recipes below call for.

You can store the purees and blends in the fridge for up to 3 days and in the freezer for up to 3 months. Missy recommends stashing them in quarter-cup sizes so you won't have to worry about defrosting too much or too little when you're ready to use them.

Make-Ahead Recipe #1: Purple Puree

3 cups raw baby spinach
leaves*

1½ cups fresh or frozen
blueberries, no syrup
or sugar added

½ teaspoon lemon juice

1 to 2 tablespoons water

*Note: I prefer raw baby
spinach to frozen spinach
for this recipe (more mild
flavor); if you use frozen
spinach, only use 1 cup of it.*

Raw baby spinach should be well rinsed, even if the package says "prewashed." If you're using frozen blueberries, give them a quick rinse under cold water to thaw a little, and then drain.

Place the spinach in the food processor first and pulse a few times. This will reduce it significantly. Next add the blueberries, lemon juice, and 1 tablespoon of water; puree on high until as smooth as possible. Stop occasionally to push the contents to the bottom. If necessary, use another tablespoon of water to create a smooth puree.

This recipe makes about 1 cup of puree. Purple puree will keep in the refrigerator up to 3 days, or you can freeze ¼-cup portions in sealed plastic bags or small plastic containers, and store for 3 months.

Purple Puree is used in the following recipes:

Chocolate Champion Cereal Cookies

Purple Power Pops

Honey BBQ Chicken Nuggets

Make-Ahead Recipe #2: Orange Puree

1 medium sweet
   potato or yam,
   peeled and coarsely
   chopped
3 medium to large
   carrots, peeled
   and sliced into
   thick chunks
2 to 3 tablespoons
   water

Place the sweet potatoes and carrots in a medium-sized pot and cover with cold water. Bring to a boil and cook for about 20 minutes, until carrots are very tender. Careful—if the carrots aren't tender enough, they may leave telltale little nuggets of vegetable in recipes, which will reveal their presence to your kids, a gigantic no-no for The Sneaky Chef.

Drain the carrots and sweet potatoes and put them in the food processor with 2 tablespoons of water. Puree on high until completely smooth—until no pieces of vegetable show. Stop occasionally to push the contents to the bottom. If necessary, use another tablespoon of water to smooth out the puree, but the less water, the better.

This recipe makes about 2 cups of puree. Orange Puree will keep in the refrigerator for up to 3 days, or you can freeze ¼-cup portions in sealed plastic bags or small plastic containers, and store for 3 months.

Orange Puree is used in the following recipes:

Clever Crepes

Get a Move On Muffin Soufflés

Jumping Jelly omelet

Muscle Man Maple Sausage Griddle Cakes

Breakfast Sushi

Rock n' Roll Pizza Sticks

Sneaky S'mores

Surprise-icle

Make Mine a Mac 'n Cheese Pizza

Crackle & Pop Peanut Butter Sandwich

Clever Crepes—For Dinner

Race Ya! Rice Balls

Honey BBQ Chicken Nuggets

BBQ Pulled Pork Sandwiches

Phabulous Philly Cheesesteak

Make-Ahead Recipe #3: Green Puree

2 cups raw baby
   spinach leaves*

2 cups broccoli florets,
   fresh or frozen

1 cup sweet green
   peas, frozen

2 to 3 tablespoons
   water

*Note: Missy prefers
raw baby spinach to
frozen spinach for
this recipe (more mild
flavor); if you use
frozen spinach, only
use 1 cup of it.

MAKES ABOUT 2 CUPS OF PUREE

Raw baby spinach should be well rinsed, even if the package says "prewashed."

To prepare Green Puree on the stovetop, pour about 2 inches of water into a pot with a tight-fitting lid. Put a vegetable steamer basket into the pot, add the broccoli, and steam for about 10 minutes, until very tender. Add the frozen peas to the basket for the last 2 minutes of steaming. Drain.

To prepare in the microwave, place the broccoli in a microwave-safe bowl, cover with water, and microwave on high for 8 to 10 minutes, until very tender. Add peas for last 2 minutes of cooking. Drain.

Place the spinach in the food processor first and pulse a few times. This will reduce it significantly. Next add the cooked broccoli and peas, along with 2 tablespoons of water. Puree on high until as smooth as possible. Stop occasionally to push the contents to the bottom. If necessary, use another tablespoon of water to make a smooth puree.

Green Puree will keep in the refrigerator for up to 3 days, or you can freeze ¼-cup portions in sealed plastic bags or small plastic containers, and store for 3 months.

Green Puree is used in the following recipes:

Phabulous Philly Cheese Steak   Beefed-Up Barley Soup

Make-Ahead Recipe #4: White Puree

2 cups cauliflower florets
(about half a small head)

2 small to medium
zucchini, peeled and
coarsely chopped

1 teaspoon fresh lemon
juice

1 to 2 tablespoons water,
if necessary

MAKES ABOUT 2 CUPS OF PUREE

To prepare White Puree on the stovetop, pour about 2 inches of water into a pot with a tight-fitting lid. Put a vegetable steamer basket into the pot, add the cauliflower, and steam for about 10 minutes, until very tender. Drain.

To prepare in the microwave, place the cauliflower in a microwave-safe bowl, cover it with water, and microwave on high for 8 to 10 minutes or until very tender. Drain.

Meanwhile, place the raw peeled zucchini with the lemon juice in your food processor and pulse a few times. Next add the cooked cauliflower and 1 tablespoon of water to the food processor (work in batches if necessary) and puree on high until smooth. Stop occasionally to push the contents to the bottom. If necessary, use another tablespoon of water to make a smooth puree, but the less water, the better.

White Puree will keep in the refrigerator for up to 3 days, or you can freeze ¼-cup portions in sealed plastic bags or small plastic containers, and store for 3 months.

White Puree is used in the following recipes:

Breakfast Pan Pizza

Cheese Fun-Do

Phabulous Philly Cheese Steak

Intro to Hummus

Chicken Noodle Salad

Top Dog Corn Muffins

Make Mine a Mac 'n' Cheese Pizza

Hot Doggitos

Clever Crepes—For Dinner

Spaghetti Fit-Tatta

Sneaky Panini

Off the Couch Potato Skins

Race ya Rice Balls

Make-Ahead Recipe #5: Strawberry Puree

2½ cups fresh or frozen
   strawberries,* no syrup
   or sugar added
½ teaspoon lemon juice
1 to 2 tablespoons water

*Try to use organic
strawberries, since they
rank high on the "dirty
dozen" list of produce
most contaminated with
pesticide residues.

MAKES ABOUT 1 CUP

Combine the strawberries, lemon juice, and 1 tablespoon of water in the bowl of a food processor and puree on high until as smooth as possible. Stop occasionally to push the contents to the bottom. If necessary, use another tablespoon of water to smooth out the puree.

Strawberry Puree will keep in the refrigerator up to 3 days, or you can freeze ¼-cup portions in sealed plastic bags or small plastic containers.

Strawberry Puree (or strawberries) is used in the following recipes:

Rainbow Pancakes with Warm
Strawberry Syrup
Sparkling Strawberry Float

Super Sports Cubes
Cold Buster
Sweet Strawberry Cupcakes

Make-Ahead Recipe #6: Cherry Puree

2½ cups fresh or frozen
    cherries,* no syrup or
    sugar added

½ teaspoon lemon juice

1 to 2 tablespoons water

Try to use organic cherries, since they rank high on the "dirty dozen" list of produce most contaminated with pesticide residues.

MAKES ABOUT 1 CUP

Combine the cherries, lemon juice, and 1 tablespoon of water in the bowl of your food processor and puree on high until as smooth as possible. Stop occasionally to push the contents to the bottom. If necessary, use another tablespoon of water to smooth-out the puree.

This recipe makes about 1 cup of puree; double it if you want to store another cup. It will keep in the refrigerator up to 3 days, or you can freeze ¼-cup portions in sealed plastic bags or small plastic containers, and store for 3 months.

Cherry Puree is used in the following recipes:

Chocolate No-Ache Shake

Black Forest Cupcakes

BBQ Pulled Pork

Gold-Medal Graham Crackers
    with Chocolate Cream Dip

Make-Ahead Recipe #7: White Bean Puree

1 (15-ounce) can white
beans* (Great Northern,
navy, butter, or
cannellini)

1 to 2 tablespoons water

*If you prefer to use dried
beans, soak overnight and
cook as directed*

MAKES ABOUT 1 CUP

Rinse and drain the beans and place them in the bowl of your food processor. Add 1 tablespoon of the water, then pulse on high until you have a smooth puree. If necessary, use a little more water, a tiny bit at a time, until the mixture smoothes out and no pieces or full beans are visible.

White Bean Puree will keep in the refrigerator for up to 3 days, or you can freeze ¼-cup portions in sealed plastic bags or small plastic containers, and store for 3 months.

White Bean Puree is used in the following recipes:

Sneaker-Doodle Cookies
Supercharged Tuna Sliders

Make-Ahead Recipe #8: Flour Blend

1 cup all-purpose,
    unbleached white flour

1 cup whole-wheat flour

1 cup wheat germ,
    unsweetened

MAKES ABOUT 3 CUPS

Combine the flours and wheat germ in a large bowl.

Flour Blend can be stored in a sealed, labeled plastic bag or container in the refrigerator for up to 3 months.

Quick Tip!

A quick replacement for my Flour Blend is whole-grain pastry flour. It's still whole grain, but very finely milled for better taste, color, and texture.

Flour Blend is used in the following recipes:

Clever Crepes

Chocolate Champion Cereal Cookies

Rainbow Pancakes with Warm
    Strawberry Syrup

Muscle Man Maple Sausage Griddle Cakes

Sneaky S'Mores

Sneaker-Doodle Cookies

Top Dog Corn Muffins

Clever Crepes—for Dinner

Make-Ahead Recipe #9: Ground Almonds

1 cup almonds, slivered and blanched

Pulse the almonds in a food processor. Don't let the food processor run continually, or you will end up with nut butter. You are aiming for a fairly coarse consistency.

This makes about two-thirds of a cup of ground almonds. Keep refrigerated in a sealed, labeled plastic bag for up to 2 weeks.

Ground Almonds are used in the following recipes:

Go-Go Granola

Make-Ahead Recipe #10: Ground Walnuts

1 cup shelled walnut halves
or pieces

Pulse the walnuts in a food processor. Don't let the food processor run continually, or you will end up with nut butter. You are aiming for a fairly coarse consistency.

This makes about two-thirds of a cup of ground walnuts. Keep refrigerated in a sealed, labeled plastic bag for up to 2 weeks.

Ground Walnuts are used in the following recipes:

Crunchy Chocolate Clusters

Instant Supermarket Purees

Note: Some Make-Aheads are actually unwittingly prepared for you by the food industry. If you find yourself short on time, or if you're in the midst of a recipe and you don't have a Make-Ahead on hand, some purees used in this book can substituted with baby foods.

MAKE AHEAD	INGREDIENTS	INSTANT SUBSTITUTE
White Puree	cauliflower, zucchini	baby food zucchini
Orange Puree	sweet potatoes, carrots	baby food sweet potatoes and carrots
Green Puree	peas, broccoli, spinach	baby food peas, spinach, vegetables
Purple Puree	blueberries, spinach	baby food apples and blueberries with baby food spinach
White Bean Puree	white beans	vegetarian refried pinto beans (these are darker in color, and not as bland as white beans—they work only with darker meat and tomato sauce)
Cherry Puree	cherries	blueberry/apple baby food
Flour Blend	flour, wheat germ	Whole-grain pastry flour

Other useful instant supermarket purees: tomato paste, applesauce, unsweetened fruit spread, and fresh, ripe avocados (mashed).

Appendix

TOYS THAT HAVE GET-UP-AND-GO!

Commercial games and toys can have your kids flexing their muscles, moving their bodies, and testing their coordination, all without it seeming like exercise. Some products fulfill the Sneaky Fitness mission more than others, and we've listed some of our favorites here. (These toys can be found at major toy stores and other retailers). Each toy is rated according to how active a child will be when playing with it. One "jumping jack" is mildy active and four "jumping jacks" means it's incredibly active. Let this list inspire you on your next trip to the toy store.

PRESCHOOLERS

• **Super Skipper** ®

 Kids jump to music around a pole that's attached to an electronic base.

• **Par 3 Mini Golf Course®**

A miniature golf game that allows kids to sink the ball around different obstacles.

• **Egg and Spoon Race**

Kids balance beanbag eggs on the spoons and race to the finish (includes 4 spoons, 4 egg shaped bean bags and 4 re-breakable shells).

• **Cranium Hullabaloo®**

Players move from one colorful pad to another and use their bodies to perform different moves, like touching your nose to a circle-shaped pad or spinning to a red one.

• **Tinkerbell's Learn Ballet Step-By-**

 **Step®**

This DVD instructs your child how to stretch properly and perform basic ballet steps. It also provides a full dance routine.

 • **Kids On Stage®**

Charades for preschoolers!

 • **Indoor Hopscotch**

A cool carpet that allows your kids to hopscotch indoors. (Includes 3 themed beanbags)

 • **I Can Play Bowling®**

A great indoor or outdoor bowling game that introduces your kids to the sport.

 • **Alex Monster Clompers®**

A cuter version of those old coffee can stilts, they're made of foam rubber so kids can stomp everywhere.

- **Radio Flyer Inchworm®**

Kids bounce on an ergonomic saddle to make the inchworm move forward.

GRADE-SCHOOLERS

- **Scavenger Hunt® for Kids**

A board game that sends kids searching for everyday items they can find all over the house.

- **Kite Dynamics®**

Kids can design, build, and fly their own unique kites.

- **Fun Roller Giant Rolling Toy**

A giant, inflatable roller that kids can actually get inside of is sure to provide energetic outdoor fun.

- **Gymnic Hop Balls®**

Your kids will love bouncing around on these fun, colorful favorites.

- **Flying Turtle®**

With this speedy basic go-cart, kids can fly fast indoors and out while maneuvering with their feet.

- **Bounty Hunter Junior Metal Detector**

A metal detector just for kids, this toy will provide hours of fun at the beach or park—and may even turn up some buried treasure!

- **Wild Planet Hyper Dash®**

A fast-paced game that includes one electronic "tagger" and five targets that kids must tag when instructed. Spread the targets around your yard or living room and watch them race from one to the other.

• The Wobbler®

Kids stand on a rounded, plastic tray and use their legs and feet to wobble 3 colored balls into the holes.

• Giant Kick Croquet Set®

Like croquet game only better! Instead of mallets, kids use their feet to kick super-sized balls through big wickets for easier, more active play.

TWEENS

• Dueling Blast Pad®

Two kids jump on pads to release their foam rockets into the air. See whose go farthest!

• Fun Ride Deluxe®

A cable line and trolley that lets kids glide, airborne.

• Nintendo Wii®

This is not the videogame of your youth! In most of these games, kids must actually perform the moves that they want their on-screen character to do.

• Dance, Dance Revolution®

Kids dance on a pad, following along with the steps on the television screen.

• Ogosport® Disc Set

Two inflatable rings with elastic mesh are used to play catch and launch balls or water balloons.

• **Aquapac® 515 MB3**

Underwater MP3 player case and headphones that'll have your children swimming for hours.

• **ME 2®**

A hand-held and online game that's powered by your kids' physical activity— the more they move, the more points they earn.

• **Hasbro Twister Moves®**

A dance version of the classic Twister game that includes 3 CDs and 144 jamming tunes.

Sneaky Fitness Activities by Category

ACTIVITIES FOR PRESCHOOLERS

#1: Marching Band

#2: Dig to China!

#3: Window Washer

#4: Parachute Party

#5: Balloon Bash

#6: The Big Bailout

#7: Bubble Bobble

#8: Wave Tag

#9: Huff and Puff

#10: Sock Hop!

#11: Get Me to the ER—STAT!

#12: Van "Go"

#13: Muscle Murals

#14: Set Up Shop

#15: Big Foot

#16: Graffiti Artist

#17: Snow Roll

#18: Rain on Your Parade

#19: Volatile Volcano

#20: Night Lights

#21: Sidewalk Art

#22: Look Ma, No Feet!

#23: Noah's Ark

#24: Fireman Drill

#25: How Many?

#26: Project Runway

#27: Ice, Ice Baby

#28: Getta Load of This!

#29: Paint the Town Red (or Blue or Green)

#30: Waitress Workout

#31: Wobble Hobble

#32: Halo Optional

#33: Fit Fort

#34: Lawn Limbo

#35: Freeze Dance

#36: Lost Toy Treasure Hunt

#37: Power Hour

#38: Mountaineers

#39: Little Miss Crabby

#40: Pound Puppy

#41: Walk This Way

#42: Pop! Pop!

#43: Get Down, Get Clean

#44: Temper Tantrum

#45: Twinkle Toes

#46: Roll with It

#47: See You Later, Alligator

#48: Smart Cookies

#49: Pick Your Own

#50: Tickle Torture

#51: Musical Chairs

#52: Couch Potato

ACTIVITIES FOR GRADE-SCHOOLERS

#8: Wave Tag

#10: Sock Hop!

#11: Get Me to the ER—STAT!

#12: Van "Go"

#13: Muscle Murals

#14: Set Up Shop

#15: Big Foot

#16: Graffiti Artist

#17: Snow Roll

#18: Rain on Your Parade

#19: Volatile Volcano

#20: Night Lights

#21: Sidewalk Art

#22: Look Ma, No Feet!

#23: Noah's Ark

#24: Fireman Drill

#25: How Many?

#26: Project Runway

#27: Ice, Ice Baby

#28: Getta Load of This!

#29: Paint the Town Red (or Blue or Green)

#30: Waitress Workout

#31: Wobble Hobble

#32: Halo Optional

#33: Fit Fort

#34: Lawn Limbo

#35: Freeze Dance

#36: Lost Toy Treasure Hunt

#37: Power Hour

#38: Mountaineers

#39: Little Miss Crabby

#40: Pound Puppy

#41: Walk This Way

#42: Pop! Pop!

#43: Get Down, Get Clean

#44: Temper Tantrum

#45: Twinkle Toes

#46: Roll with It

#47: See You Later, Alligator

#48: Smart Cookies

#49: Pick Your Own

#50: Tickle Torture

#51: Musical Chairs

#52: Couch Potato

#53: No-Skate Hockey

#54: The Amazing Race

#55: Go Carts

#56: Showtime!

#57: Slap Shot!

#58: So You Wanna Be a Rock Star?

#59: Just Bag It

#60: Hip Hop

#61: Backyard Bowling

#62: Walk Like an Italian

#63: Bus Stop Hop

#64: Obstacle Course

#65: Little Red Wagon

#66: Baby You Can Drive This Car

#67: Chore Time!

#68: Green Thumbs

#69: Go Green

#70: Your American Idol

#71: Top Chef

#72: Make a Splash!

#73: Search & Dive

#74: Surreptitious Charades

#75: Little Squirts

#76: Sneaky Southpaw

#77: Basket Cases

#78: On a Roll

#79: Slip and Slide

#80: Main Squeeze

#81: Community Clean Up

#82: Sneaky Shoelaces

#83: Pillow Fight!

#84: I'm With the Band

#85: Anything You Can Do, I Can Do Better

#86: Throw for Distance

#87: Bounce, Bounce, Bounce

#88: Memory Moves

#89: Wake-Up Call

#90: Remote Control

#91: Homework High-Five

#92: Halftime Show

#93: Loch Ness Monster

ACTIVITIES FOR TWEENS

#27: Ice, Ice Baby

#28: Getta Load of This!

#29: Paint the Town Red (or Blue or Green)

#30: Waitress Workout

#31: Wobble Hobble

#32: Halo Optional

#33: Fit Fort

#34: Lawn Limbo

#35: Freeze Dance

#36: Lost Toy Treasure Hunt

#37: Power Hour

#38: Mountaineers

#39: Little Miss Crabby

#40: Pound Puppy

#41: Walk This Way

#42: Pop! Pop!

#43: Get Down, Get Clean

#44: Temper Tantrum

#45: Twinkle Toes

#46: Roll with It

#47: See You Later, Alligator

#48: Smart Cookies

#49: Pick Your Own

#50: Tickle Torture

#51: Musical Chairs

#52: Couch Potato

#57: Slap Shot!

#58: So You Wanna Be a Rock Star?

#59: Just Bag It

#60: Hip Hop

#61: Backyard Bowling

#62: Walk Like an Italian

#63: Bus Stop Hop

#64: Obstacle Course

#65: Little Red Wagon

#66: Baby You Can Drive This Car

#67: Chore Time!

#68: Green Thumbs

#69: Go Green

#70: Your American Idol

#71: Top Chef

#72: Make a Splash!

#73: Search & Dive

#74: Surreptitious Charades

#75: Little Squirts

#76: Sneaky Southpaw

#77: Basket Cases

#78: On a Roll

#79: Slip and Slide

#80: Main Squeeze

#81: Community Clean Up

#82: Sneaky Shoelaces

#83: Pillow Fight!

#84: I'm With the Band

#85: Anything You Can Do, I Can Do Better

#86: Throw for Distance

#87: Bounce, Bounce, Bounce

#88: Memory Moves

#89: Wake-Up Call

#90: Remote Control

#91: Homework High-Five

#92: Halftime Show

#93: Loch Ness Monster

#94: Purchasing Power

#95: It's a Beautiful Day in the Neighborhood

#96: Adopt a Cause

#97: Suds 'R' Us

#98: Job Joy

#99: Walk the Walk, Talk the Talk

#100: Sneaky Fitness Home Edition

ANY DAY ACTIVITIES

#1: Marching Band

#4: Parachute Party

#9: Huff and Puff

#10: Sock Hop!

#11: Get Me to the ER—STAT!

#12: Van "Go"

#13: Muscle Murals

#22: Look Ma, No Feet!

#25: How Many?

#26: Project Runway

#27: Ice, Ice Baby

#28: Getta Load of This!

#30: Waitress Workout

#35: Freeze Dance

#36: Lost Toy Treasure Hunt

#42: Pop! Pop!

#44: Temper Tantrum

#45: Twinkle Toes

#47: See You Later, Alligator

#48: Smart Cookies

#55: Go Carts

#56: Showtime!

#58: So You Wanna Be a Rock Star?

#59: Just Bag It

#67: Chore Time!

#69: Go Green

#70: Your American Idol

#71: Top Chef

#74: Surreptitious Charades

#76: Sneaky Southpaw

WEEKEND ACTIVITIES

PLAYDATE ACTIVITIES

#1: Marching Band

#5: Balloon Bash

#11: Get Me to the ER—STAT!

#13: Muscle Murals

#14: Set Up Shop

#16: Graffiti Artist

#18: Snow Roll

#19: Volatile Volcano

#22: Sidewalk Art

#23: Noah's Ark

#26: Project Runway

#27: Ice, Ice, Baby

#29: Paint the Town Red (or Blue or Green)

#31: Wobble Hobble

#32: Halo Optional

#33: Fit Fort

#34: Lawn Limbo

#35: Freeze Dance

#48: Smart Cookies

#49: Pick Your Own

#53: No-Skate Hockey

#56: Showtime!

#57: Slap Shot!

#58: So You Wanna Be a Rock Star?

#61: Backyard Bowling

#64: Obstacle Course

#70: Your American Idol

#71: Top Chef

#72: Make a Splash!

#73: Search & Dive

#74: Surreptitious Charades

#75: Little Squirts

#83: Pillow Fight!

#86: Throw for Distance

#97: Suds 'R' Us

PARTY ACTIVITIES

#1: Marching Band

#5: Balloon Bash

#23: Noah's Ark

#31: Wobble Hobble

#35: Freeze Dance

#58: So You Wanna Be a Rock Star?

#70: Your American Idol

#73: Search & Dive

#74: Surreptitious Charades

#83: Pillow Fight!

SUNNY DAY ACTIVITIES

#2: Dig to China!

#3: Window Washer

#5: Balloon Bash

#6: The Big Bailout

#7: Bubble Bobble

#8: Wave Tag

RAINY DAY ACTIVITIES

SNOWY DAY ACTIVITIES

#15: Big Foot

#16: Graffiti Artist

#18: Snow Roll

#32: Halo Optional

#33: Fit Fort

EVERY DAY ACTIVITIES

#20: Night Lights

#24: Fireman Drill

#38: Mountaineers

#40: Pound Puppy

#43: Get Down, Get Clean

#51: Musical Chairs

#52: Couch Potato

#54: The Amazing Race

#60: Hip Hop

#62: Walk Like an Italian

#63: Bus Stop Hop

#82: Sneaky Shoelaces

#88: Memory Moves

#89: Wake-Up Call

#90: Remote Control

#91: Homework High-Five

#92: Halftime Show

#99: Walk the Walk, Talk the Talk

Acknowledgments

We'd like to thank you, our readers, for allowing us to share our passion and our ideals for our children's good health. We hope this book has given you inspiration to add fun and fitness in your family's life, as it has ours.

This book is an extension of The Sneaky Chef family, and we've been blessed with an incredibly talented team of professionals and our own personal support systems, all of whom have helped us bring this book into your homes:

Our publishing team at The Perseus Books Group/Running Press: CEO David Steinberger, Publisher Christopher Navratil, Executive Editor Jennifer Kasius, Associate Publisher Craig Herman, Art Director Bill Jones, interior designer Alicia Freile, and the entire Running Press team. It is an honor to work with each of you and we thank you for all your support, guidance, and expertise.

Our brilliant and supportive literary agent, Joëlle Delbourgo. We're so fortunate to have you on our side!

Our phenomenal writing consultant, Molly Lyons. We appreciate all your hard work and your knack for helping us all keep a sense of humor.

Our super-talented food photographer, Jerry Errico, and five-star food stylist, Brian Preston-Campbell. You both bring The Sneaky Chef recipes to life with your work. (Not to mention how much fun we have together on those shoots!)

Our designers. A special thanks goes to Kris Weber of A/W Design who created The Sneaky Chef and Sneaky Fitness logos that we all have come to know and love. We're also honored to showcase the artistic talent of Rachel Arseneau, who created the adorable nutritional and fitness icons.

Our brilliant consultants: Brigitte Miner, Laurence Chase, Karen Ganz, Carol Chase, Sharon Hammer, and Ken and Brenda Fritz. We value your expertise and your endless contributions. We sincerely appreciate the generous advice and guidance of one of America's Best Pediatricians, Max Kahn, MD, psychotherapist, Susan F. Schrott, LCSW and the expert nutritional consulting and recipe analyses by Stacey B. Schulman,

MS, RD, CDN, Registered Dietitian. We are grateful to our invaluable book consultant, Amanita Rosenbush, whose expertise and advice helps create bestsellers.

Our families and dear friends are our support systems. Thank you for your overall encouragement and confidence in us. Sneaky Chef recipes would not taste as delicious without the culinary expertise and guidance of Missy's stepmother, Ulla Chase. She thanks you and her father for all their love and support. Missy also thanks her husband Rick Lapine, and her girls, Samantha and Emily. She is eternally grateful for their love and support.

Larysa is thankful for her parents for always supporting their hardworking daughter, and her husband, Steven DiDio, and her kids, Nicholas and Isabella, for their never-ending love, support and priceless contributions.

Dear Readers,

Thank you for sharing your time with us, and for making Sneaky Fitness and The Sneaky Chef a part of your life. To share your ideas and comments, and for new recipes, tips, special promotions, and appearance dates, please come visit us at:

www.TheSneakyChef.com/SneakyFitness

In good health, from our families to yours,
Missy and Larysa

Recipe Index

Make-Ahead Recipes Index

Notes

Notes

Notes

Notes

Notes